Contents

Module 1 1

Module 2 17

Module 3 35

Module 4 54

Module 5 71

Module 6 86

Module 7 103

Module 8 119

Module 9 137

Module 10 151

Module 11 166

Module 12 181

Module 13 196

Module 14 211

Module 15 226

Module 16 242

Module 17 260

Module 18 276

Sight Words 293

© 2020 by Accelerate Education
Visit us on the Web at: www.accelerate.education

My Adventures

1.1 Journal Entry

skydiving

Name _____.

Directions: Write your response to the prompt on the lines below. Don't forget to check for complete sentences as you write.

Prompt: What if you could fly for just one day? What kind of adventures would you have?

_____
_____
_____
_____
_____
_____
_____
_____
_____
_____
_____
_____
_____
_____
_____
_____

1.1 - My Adventures

1.2 Spelling Worksheet

Name _____

Alphabetical Order

Directions: Your spelling words are listed in the word bank. Please write them in alphabetical order on the lines below.

1) _____
2) _____
3) _____
4) _____
5) _____
6) _____
7) _____
8) _____
9) _____
10) _____
11) _____
12) _____
13) _____
14) _____
15) _____
16) _____
17) _____
18) _____
19) _____
20) _____

Word Bank:

and, away, big, blue, can, come, down, find, for, funny, go, flag, crab, sled, drip, trim, clog, flop, drum, club

My Adventures

Name _____.

Incomplete Thought to Complete Sentence

Directions:
Make each of the following groups of words a complete sentence by adding a subject, a predicate or both.

Example: in the summer
I play baseball in the summer.

1) run around the yard

2) my little brother

3) the dog next door

4) rides a bicycle

5) at the park

1.2 - My Adventures

Personal Narrative Prewrite

Topic Sentence: _____

Details
What happened? _____
When? _____
Where? _____
Who was there? _____

○○○ **Beginning**

```
_____
_____
_____
```

○●○ **Middle**

```
_____
_____
_____
```

○○● **End**

```
_____
_____
_____
```

Conclusion: _____

My Adventures

1.2 Handwriting Practice

Name _____ .

c c   *c c*

a a   *a a*

d d   *d d*

g g   *g g*

c c   *c c*

a a   *a a*

d d   *d d*

g g   *g g*

1.2 - My Adventures

Name _____.

1.4 Spelling Worksheet

Fill in the Blanks

Directions: Fill in the blanks to spell each word following the **CCVC** pattern.

1)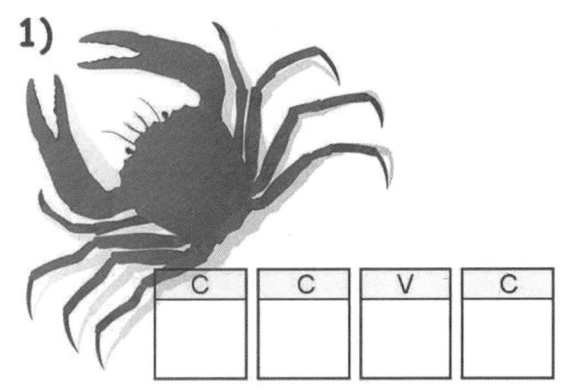

C	C	V	C

2)

C	C	V	C

3)

C	C	V	C

4)

C	C	V	C

5)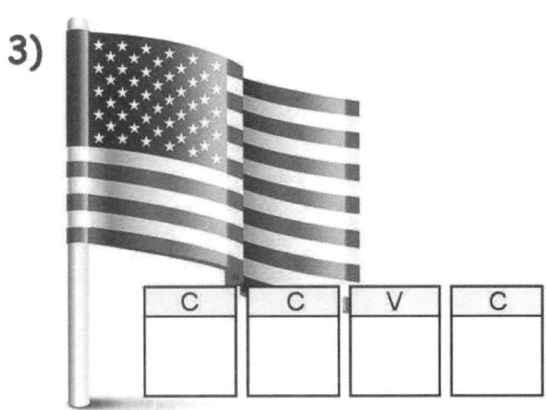

C	C	V	C

6)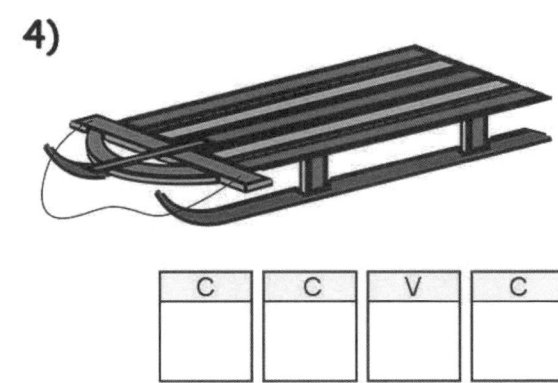

C	C	V	C

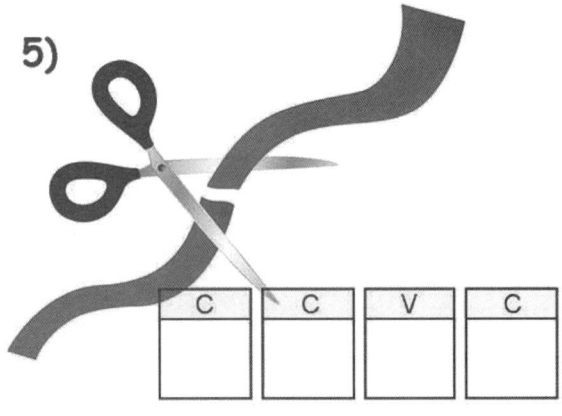

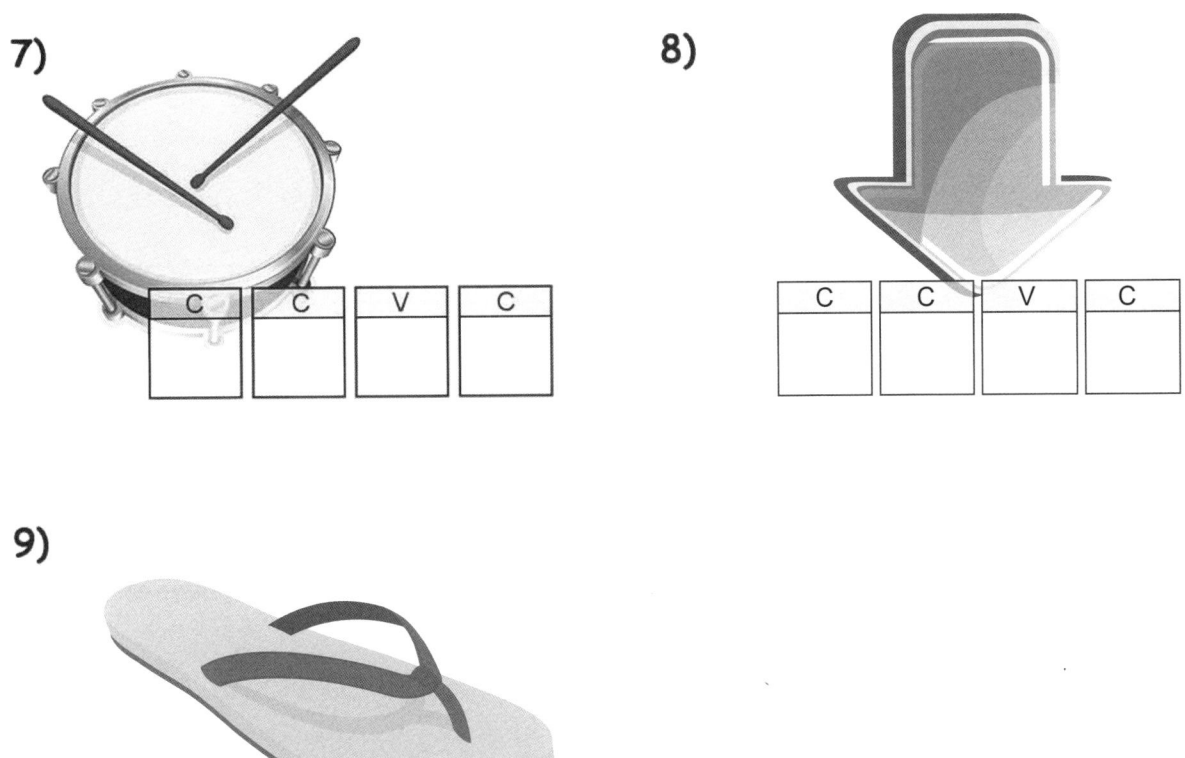

Directions: Circle the correct spelling of the word and then write that correct spelling on the line.

Circle Correct Spelling   Write Correct Word

1) straie   stray   straay   _____

2) clog   clogg   clag   _____

3) find   fiend   finde   _____

4) funne   funnie   funny   _____

5) fritten   frighton   frighten   _____

6) harness   harnes   harnness   _____

7) doun   downe   down   _____

8) come   com   cume   _____

9) awaye   away   awy   _____

10) wannder   wander   wanderr   _____

11) rompp   roomp   romp   _____

Name _____

Incomplete and Complete Sentences

Directions: Decide whether each is a complete sentence by circling complete or incomplete. If it is an incomplete sentence rewrite it into a complete sentence on the line below.

1. In my room.   Complete   Incomplete

2. With my friend.   Complete   Incomplete

3. She lost.   Complete   Incomplete

4. Hid the game.   Complete   Incomplete

1.4 - My Adventures

9

5. Ran from the dog down the street.   Complete   Incomplete

6. I took a walk.   Complete   Incomplete

7. My mom forgot.   Complete   Incomplete

8. My best friend.   Complete   Incomplete

1.4 Writing Checklist

Name _____.

Personal Narrative Checklist

Directions: Reread your writing carefully. Put a check in each box under Author as you complete each item. Once all the boxes are checked, give this to your teacher for the final edit.

Revise and Edit for the following:	Author	Teacher
1. **Clarity and Meaning** 　*Ask yourself,* 　"Will this story make sense to a stranger?" 　"Did I explain the important part?" 　Rewrite parts that need revision.		

Revise and Edit for the following:	Author	Teacher
2. **Correct Use of Words** 　*Ask yourself,* 　"Did I use specific details and words?" 　"Did I explain?" 　"Do my sentences sound good together?" 　Rewrite parts that need revision.		

Revise and Edit for the following:	Author	Teacher
3. **Capitalization** 　Use capitals at the beginning of each sentence and for every name. 　Make corrections if needed.		

Continue on next page.

Revise and Edit for the following:	Author	Teacher

4. Punctuation
 	
    Use periods, exclamation points, and question marks.
 	
    Use quotation marks for dialogue.
 	
    Make corrections if needed.		

Revise and Edit for the following:	Author	Teacher

5. Spelling
 	
    Check for correct spelling.
 	
    Make corrections if needed.		

 **1.4 Handwriting Practice**

Name _____ .

Directions: Write each letter across the line.

Example:

c c c c c c c c c c

c

c

a

a

d

d

g

g

1.4 - My Adventures 13

My Adventures

Name _____ .

Spelling Test

1.5 Spelling Test

Directions:
As your teacher reads your words, write each spelling word on the blanks below.

1) _____   11) _____

2) _____   12) _____

3) _____   13) _____

4) _____   14) _____

5) _____   15) _____

6) _____   16) _____

7) _____   17) _____

8) _____   18) _____

9) _____   19) _____

10) _____   20) _____

1.5 Story Structure Worksheet

Reading

Name _____.

Story Structure

Directions: Complete this worksheet using information from our story from this week.

Characters _____

_____
_____

Setting _____

Details

_____
_____

Beginning ○○○

Middle ○○○

End ○○○

1.5 - My Adventures   15

My Adventures

1.5 Independent Reading

Name _____.

Independent Reading

Directions: Read your independent reading book for 30 minutes. When you are done, write a few sentences explaining what you read. What happened in your story or what did you learn?

I read _____ by _____
         (book title)   (author)

for 30 minutes today.

_____   _____
       My Signature   Parent/Guardian Signature

Details

What happened in your story today or what did you learn?

_____

_____

_____

_____

_____

_____

16   1.5 - My Adventures

Space Adventures

Name _____

2.1 Journal Entry

Directions: Write your response to the prompt on the lines below. Don't forget to check for complete sentences as you write.

Prompt: What if you could travel to the moon? What would you see? What would you do?

_____
_____
_____
_____
_____
_____
_____
_____
_____
_____
_____
_____
_____
_____
_____
_____
_____

Space Adventures

2.2 Spelling Worksheet

Name _____.

Fill in the Blanks

Directions: Fill in the blanks to spell each word following the **CVCe** pattern.

1)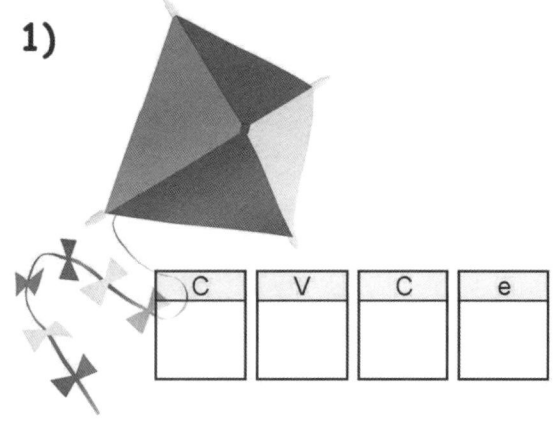

C	V	C	e

2)

C	V	C	e

3)

C	V	C	e

4)

C	V	C	e

5)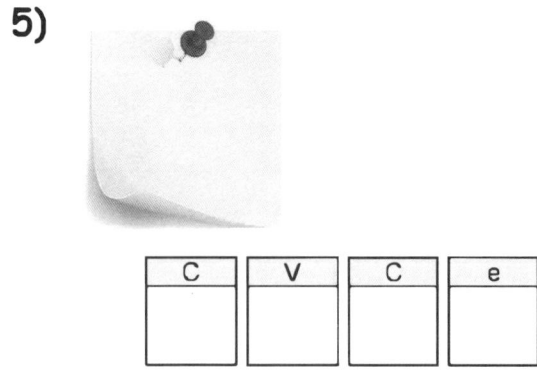

C	V	C	e

6)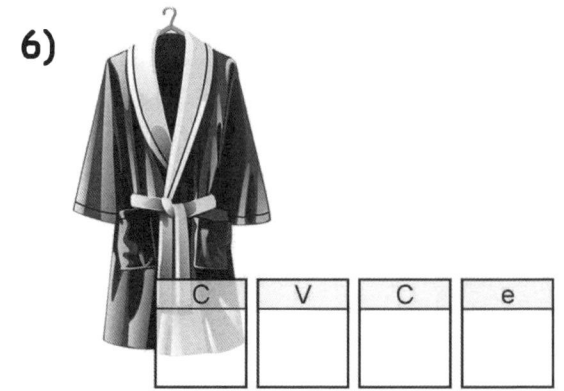

C	V	C	e

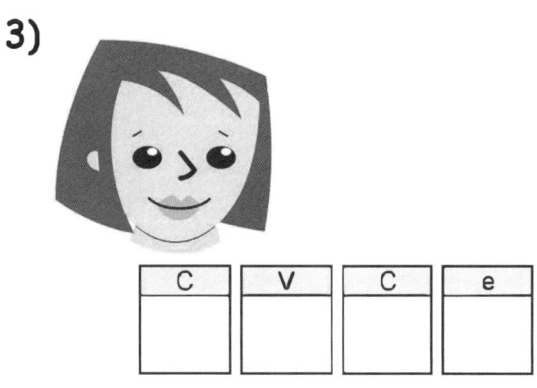

7)

C	V	C	e

8)

C	V	C	e

Directions: Write each spelling word two times.

1) help _____ _____

2) here _____ _____

3) I _____ _____

4) in _____ _____

5) is _____ _____

6) it _____ _____

7) jump _____ _____

8) little _____ _____

9) look _____ _____

10) make _____ _____

11) me _____ _____

12) my _____ _____

2.2 - Space Adventures

Space Adventures

Name _____.

2.2 Reading KWL

Reading

Reading KWL

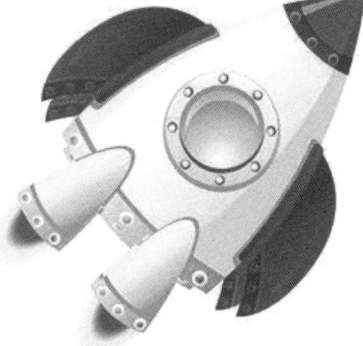

Directions:

Details

Before Reading
- Fill out the K section with what you already know about space.
- Fill out the W section with what you would like to know about space.

After Reading
- Fill out the L section with what you learned.

K
W
L

20 2.2 - Space Adventures

 **Space Adventures**  **2.2 Handwriting Practice**

Name _____ .

Directions: Use the lines to help write each letter on the first line and continue writing each letter on your own on the second line.

Example

2.3 Spelling Worksheet

Name _____.

Long Vowel Sounds

Directions:
Sort the spelling words in the Word Bank based on their long vowel sound.

WORD BANK:
cute   cave   mice   note
robe   rule   face   kite

Long **a**	Long **i**	Long **o**	Long **u**

Directions: Write each spelling word two times.

1) help _____ _____

2) here _____ _____

3) I _____ _____

4) in _____ _____

5) is _____ _____

6) it _____ _____

7) jump _____ _____

Continue on next page.

22   2.3 - Space Adventures

8) little _____ _____

9) look   _____ _____

10) make   _____ _____

11) me   _____ _____

11) my   _____ _____

2.3 Vocabulary Crossword

Name _____.

Directions: Use the definitions to complete the crossword puzzle using your vocabulary words.

Across:

5. a star with a group of planets, moons, asteroids, and comets that orbit it

6. the force that pulls down on all objects on Earth

Down:

1. to search through

2. to move in a circle around

3. groups of stars that form a pattern

4. the region beyond Earth's atmosphere

24   2.3 - Space Adventures

2.3 Reading Graphic Organizer

Name _____.

Directions: As you read the text, write down the main idea and details.

Main Idea: _____

Detail:

Detail:

Detail:

2.3 - Space Adventures

Name _____.

Grammar: Punctuation

Directions: Decide whether the sentence is making a statement, asking a question, or expressing emotion. Add the proper punctuation to the end.

1) There are 33 students in my class_____

2) What time does class start_____

3) The house is on fire_____

4) The shop on the corner sells notebooks and paper_____

5) My dad said he is going to double my allowance_____

6) Why aren't you coming on the trip_____

7) How long will it take us to get to the museum_____

8) I returned the books to the library_____

9) Where is the office_____

10) What is your favorite sport_____

11) James scored his first winning touchdown_____

12) Is Emily your best friend_____

26   2.3 - Space Adventures

Name _____.

Spelling Word Sentences

Directions:
Use each of your spelling words in a sentence.

1) help _____

2) here _____

3) I _____

4) in _____

5) is _____

6) it _____

7) jump _____

8) little _____

9) look _____

10) make _____

2.4 - Space Adventures

11) me _____

12) my _____

13) face _____

14) cave _____

15) mice _____

16) kite _____

17) robe _____

18) note _____

19) cute _____

20) rule _____

Name _____.

Declarative, Interrogative and Exclamatory

Directions:
Write whether each sentence below is **declarative**, **interrogative** or **exclamatory**.

1) I went to the store.  _____

2) Did you remember to buy milk? _____

3) I paid the cashier.  _____

4) The cashier forgot my change! _____

Punctuation

Directions: Add the correct punctuation to the end of each sentence.

1) The store was out of butter_____

2) I spilled the milk all over the floor_____

3) Can I help clean up the mess_____

4) Do you have a mop_____

5) I need to call my mom_____

6) Can I borrow your phone_____

2.4 - Space Adventures

29

Space Adventures

Name _____

2.4 Writing Checklist

Summary Checklist

Directions: Reread your writing carefully. Put a check in each box under Author as you complete each item. Once all the boxes are checked, give this to your teacher for the final edit.

Revise and Edit for the following:	Author	Teacher
1. Clarity and Meaning 　*Ask yourself,* 　"Will this summary make sense to someone who hasn't read the full text?" 　"Did I include enough details to support the main idea?" 　Rewrite parts that need revision.		

Revise and Edit for the following:	Author	Teacher
2. Correct Use of Words 　*Ask yourself,* 　"Did I use specific details and words?" 　"Did I explain?" 　"Do my sentences sound good together?" 　Rewrite parts that need revision.		

Revise and Edit for the following:	Author	Teacher
3. Capitalization 　Use capitals at the beginning of each sentence and for every name. 　Make corrections if needed.		

Continue on next page.

Revise and Edit for the following:	Author	Teacher
4. **Punctuation** Use periods, exclamation points, and question marks. Use quotation marks for dialogue. Make corrections if needed.		

Revise and Edit for the following:	Author	Teacher
5. **Spelling** Check for correct spelling. Make corrections if needed.		

 **Handwriting Practice**

Name _____.

Directions: Write each letter across the line as shown.

Example:

h h h h h h h h

h

h

t

t

p

p

2.4 - Space Adventures

Name _____

Spelling Test

Directions: As your teacher reads your words, write each spelling word on the blanks below.

1) _____ 11) _____

2) _____ 12) _____

3) _____ 13) _____

4) _____ 14) _____

5) _____ 15) _____

6) _____ 16) _____

7) _____ 17) _____

8) _____ 18) _____

9) _____

10) _____

2.5 - Space Adventures

Independent Reading

Name _____.

Independent Reading

Directions: Read your independent reading book for 30 minutes. When you are done, write a few sentences explaining what you read. What happened in your story or what did you learn?

I read _____ by _____
          (book title)   (author)

for 30 minutes today.

_____   _____
     My Signature   Parent/Guardian Signature

Details

What happened in your story today or what did you learn?

_____
_____
_____
_____
_____
_____
_____

2.5 - Space Adventures

Name _____

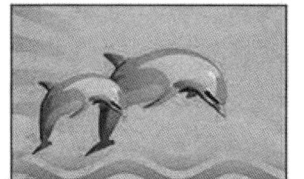

Journal Entry

Directions: Write your response to the prompt on the lines below. Don't forget to check for complete sentences as you write.

Prompt: Imagine that you have found a message in a bottle washed up on the beach. What does the message say? Where do you think it's from? What would you do with it?

_____
_____
_____
_____
_____
_____
_____
_____
_____
_____
_____
_____
_____
_____
_____
_____

3.1 - Ocean Adventures

Ocean Adventures

3.2 Spelling Worksheet

Name _____.

Long Vowel Sounds

Directions:
Sort the spelling words in the Word Bank based on their long vowel sound.

WORD BANK:
nail   meat   suit   road
read   float   blue   rain

Long a	Long e	Long o	Long u

Directions: Write each sight word two times.

1) not _____ _____

2) one _____ _____

3) play _____ _____

4) red _____ _____

5) run _____ _____

6) said _____ _____

7) see _____ _____

Continue on the next page.

3.2 - Ocean Adventures

8) the _____ _____

9) three _____ _____

10) to _____ _____

11) two _____ _____

12) up _____ _____

Ocean Adventures

Name _____

How-to Paragraph Prewrite

3.2 Writing Graphic Organizer

Directions: Write your topic for your how-to paragraph on the line below. Then, write your steps in the boxes.

Details

Topic: _____

Step One

Step Two

Step Three

Continue on the next page.

Step Four

Step Five

3.2 - Ocean Adventures

Handwriting Practice

Name _____.

Directions:
Use the **grey** lines to help you write each letter on the first line.
Continue writing each letter on your own on the second line.

Example:

e e e e e e e e e

e

l l l l l l l l l

l

f f f f f f f f f

f

3.2 - Ocean Adventures

Vocabulary Worksheet

Name _____.

Directions:
Use the word bank to fill in the blanks in the paragraph below.

WORD BANK:
swift   predator   magnificent
journey   coast   crew

It was time to set sail. The _____ gathered together to prepare the boat for sea. They hoisted the sails and pushed off. They were setting out on a _____ that would take them to Florida. As they sailed farther away from the _____, they could no longer see land. They sailed all day. They enjoyed watching the dolphins jump through the waves. The dolphins were so _____ in the water. They had no trouble keeping up with the boat. The people in the boat also spotted a few sharks. The sharks scared the dolphins away because the shark is a _____ of the dolphin. As the sun began to set over the ocean, they admired the _____ view. It was a beautiful sight.

3.3 - Ocean Adventures

41

Name _____.

Subjects and Predicates

Directions: For each sentence below, circle the subject and underline the predicate. They won't all be compound subjects and compound predicates. Some will be simple subjects and simple predicates.

1. My parents and I drove to the beach for the day.

2. I couldn't wait to build sandcastles and jump in the waves.

3. My mom and I walked on the beach and collected shells.

4. My dad read his book and napped in his chair.

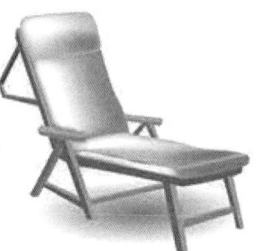

5. My dad and I built an enormous sandcastle!

6. I rode the waves on my boogie board and caught some great waves.

7. Sarah and Megan were two friends that I played with.

3.3 - Ocean Adventures

Ocean Adventures

3.4 Spelling Worksheet

Name _____.

Spelling Word Practice

Directions:
Write each of the spelling words below. Use a red colored pencil to write the consonants and a blue colored pencil to write the vowels.

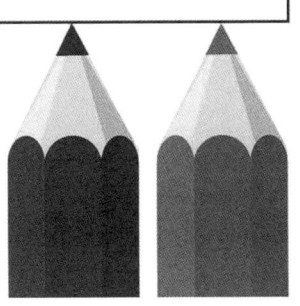

Example:
seed   seed

1) help _____
2) here _____
3) I   _____
4) in   _____
5) is   _____
6) it   _____
7) jump _____

Continue on the next page.

Directions: Circle the correct spelling of the sight word and then write the correct spelling of the sight word on the line beside it.

can

Circle Correct Spelling	Write Correct Word

1) not   noot   nowt   _____

2) wone   one   oune   _____

3) play   plae   pley   _____

4) rede   redd   red   _____

5) run   rune   ruun   _____

6) saed   sade   said   _____

7) see   se   sei   _____

8) thei   the   thee   _____

9) tou   tu   to   _____

10) two   tuo   tuu   _____

11) up   upp   upe   _____

44   3.4 - Ocean Adventures

Ocean Adventures

3.4 Grammar Worksheet

Name _____.

Subjects and Predicates

Directions:
For each sentence below, **circle the subject** and **underline the predicate**. They won't all be compound subjects and compound predicates. Some will be simple subjects and simple predicates.

1. My family and I rode on a ship last summer.

2. My sister and brother were scared of the ship.

3. I ran around the decks and looked over the edge.

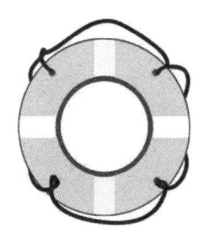

4. My mom was yelling at me not to lean over the edge.

5. My sister and I saw dolphins.

6. The dolphins were swimming and jumping in the waves.

7. I loved the trip and hope we can go again.

Continue on the next page.

Directions:
Each sentence below is missing either a subject or predicate. Follow the directions to add the missing piece and make a complete sentence.

1. _____ rode our bikes on the beach.
   (add a compound subject)

2. My best friend and I _____
   (add a compound predicate)
   at the beach.

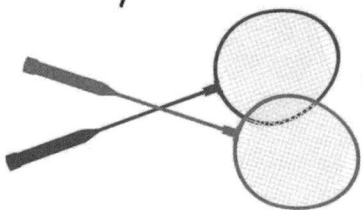

3. _____ walked back to
   (add a compound subject)
   our house.

4. My mom _____
   (add a compound predicate)
   in the ocean.

46   3.4 - Ocean Adventures

Ocean Adventures

Name _____

How-to Paragraph Checklist

3.4 Paragraph Checklist

Directions: Reread your writing carefully. Put a check in each box under Author as you complete each item. Once all the boxes are checked, your peer partner will check your paragraph and put a check in each box.

Revise and Edit for the following:	Author	Peer Partner
1. **Clarity and Meaning** **Ask yourself,** "Does the how-to paragraph explain how to do something?" "Are the steps clear and easy to follow?" Rewrite parts that need revision.		

Revise and Edit for the following:	Author	Peer Partner
2. **Correct Use of Words** **Ask yourself,** "Are specific details and words used?" "Are explanations used when needed?" "Do the sentences sound good together?" Rewrite parts that need revision.		

Revise and Edit for the following:	Author	Peer Partner
3. **Capitalization** Use capitals at the beginning of each sentence and for every name. Make corrections if needed.		

Continue on next page.

Revise and Edit for the following:	Author	Peer Partner
4. Punctuation Use periods, exclamation points, and question marks. Use quotation marks for dialogue. Make corrections if needed.		

Revise and Edit for the following:	Author	Peer Partner
5. Spelling Check for correct spelling. Make corrections if needed.		

Ocean Adventures

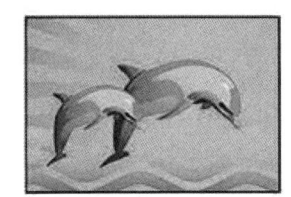

3.4 Handwriting Practice

Name _____.

Directions: Write each letter across the line as shown.

Example:

e e e e e e e e e

e

e

l

l

f

f

3.4 - Ocean Adventures

49

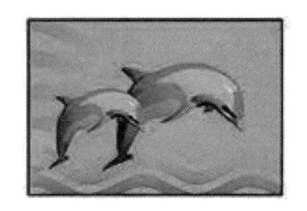

Name _____ .

Spelling Test

Directions:
As your teacher reads your words, write each spelling word on the blanks below.

1) _____   11) _____

2) _____   12) _____

3) _____   13) _____

4) _____   14) _____

5) _____   15) _____

6) _____   16) _____

7) _____   17) _____

8) _____   18) _____

9) _____   19) _____

10) _____   20) _____

Ocean Adventures

3.4 Reading Worksheet

Deep Sea Mystery

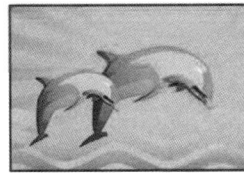

Name _____.

Directions:
Please answer the question below after reading "Deep Sea Mystery".

1. What did the crew of the ship believe Lana was doing while exploring the ocean floor?

   _____
   _____
   _____
   _____
   _____
   _____
   _____

2. What did Lana's brother Marcus believe she was doing while exploring the ocean floor?

   _____
   _____
   _____
   _____
   _____
   _____
   _____

Continue on next page.

3.5 - Ocean Adventures   51

3. **Make an inference!**
At the end of the story, Marcus says he has a pretty good idea about where Lana and her other brother are. Where do you think they are? Remember to use clues from the story to help you with your answer.

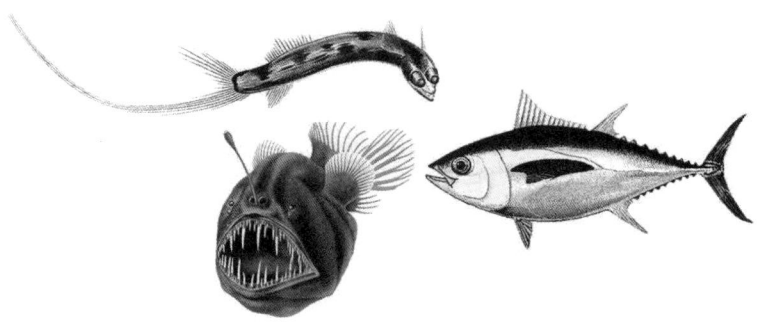

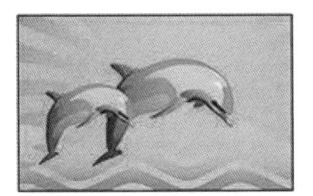

Name _____

Independent Reading

Independent Reading

Directions: Read your independent reading book for 30 minutes. When you are done, write a few sentences explaining what you read. What happened in your story or what did you learn?

I read _____ by _____
        (book title)   (author)

for 30 minutes today.

_____   _____
        My Signature   Parent/Guardian Signature

Details

What happened in your story today or what did you learn?

_____

_____

_____

_____

_____

_____

_____

3.5 - Ocean Adventures

Name _____

Journal Entry

Directions: Write your response to the prompt on the lines below. Don't forget to check for complete sentences as you write.

Prompt: Write about a time when you learned a lesson. What happened and what did you learn?

_____
_____
_____
_____
_____
_____
_____
_____
_____
_____
_____
_____
_____
_____
_____
_____

4.1 - Fables

Name _____

Rainbow Words

Directions:
Please choose three different colored pencils. Write each spelling word three times using each color.

we _____ _____ _____

where _____ _____ _____

yellow _____ _____ _____

you _____ _____ _____

all _____ _____ _____

am _____ _____ _____

are _____ _____ _____

at _____ _____ _____

ate _____ _____ _____

be _____ _____ _____

black _____ _____ _____

meet _____ _____ _____

Continue on the next page.

4.2 - Fables

deal _____ _____ _____

beach _____ _____ _____

sweet _____ _____ _____

seen _____ _____ _____

mean _____ _____ _____

queen _____ _____ _____

green _____ _____ _____

street _____ _____ _____

Name _____.

Writing Graphic Organizer

Directions: Complete this worksheet using information from our story from this week.

Characters _____
_____
_____

Setting _____
_____

Details

Beginning ○○○

Middle ○○○

End ○○○

4.2 - Fables

Handwriting Practice 1

Name _____.

Directions:
Use the grey lines to help you write each letter on the first line. Continue writing each letter on your own on the second line.

Example

u u u u u u u u

u

Example

y y y y y y y y

y

Example

i i i i i i i i

i

Example

j j j j j j j j

j

58   4.2 - Fables

Name _____.

Vocabulary Word Crossword

Directions: Use the definitions to complete the crossword puzzle using your vocabulary words.

Down:
1. a device for catching animals
2. excellent in quality or appearance
3. to bite or chew with the teeth
4. a room or set of rooms below the ground, basement

Across:
4. a closet with shelves for cups, dishes or food
5. a state of quiet

4.3 - Fables

59

Grammar Worksheet 1

Name _____

Simple and Compound Sentences

Directions: For each compound sentence below, **underline the simple sentences** and **circle the conjunction** that joins them.

Example:

The mice scurried across the floor, (and) they escaped the cat.

1. The cat ran after the mice, but she didn't catch them.

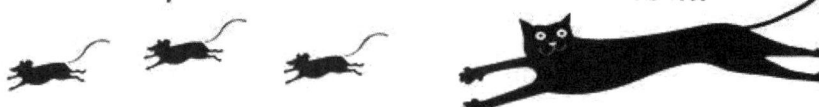

2. The mice were tired after all that running, so they had a snack.

3. The cat waited for the mice to come out of the cupboard, but she fell asleep.

4. The mice snuck past the cat, and they didn't wake her.

5. The cat woke up, but she didn't hear the mice anymore.

6. The cat searched the house for the mice, but she couldn't find them.

7. The mice were free, but they were always looking out for the cat.

4.3 - Fables

Name _____.

Spelling Worksheet

Fill in the Blanks

Directions: Fill in the blanks to spell each word following the CVVC pattern.

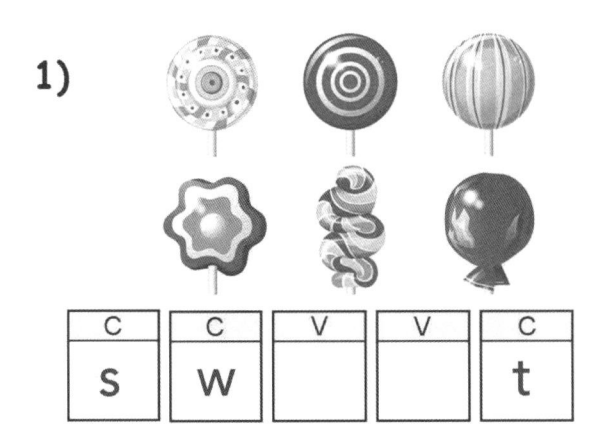

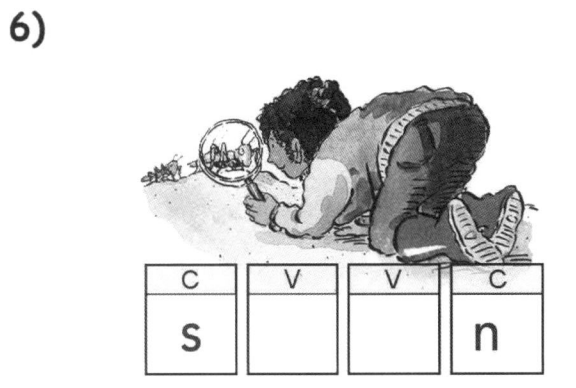

1)
C	C	V	V	C
s	w			t

2)
C	V	V	C
m			t

3)
C	V	V	C
m			n

4)
C	V	V	C
d			l

5)
C	V	V	C	C
b			c	h

6)
C	V	V	C
s			n

Continue on following page.

4.4 - Fables

7)

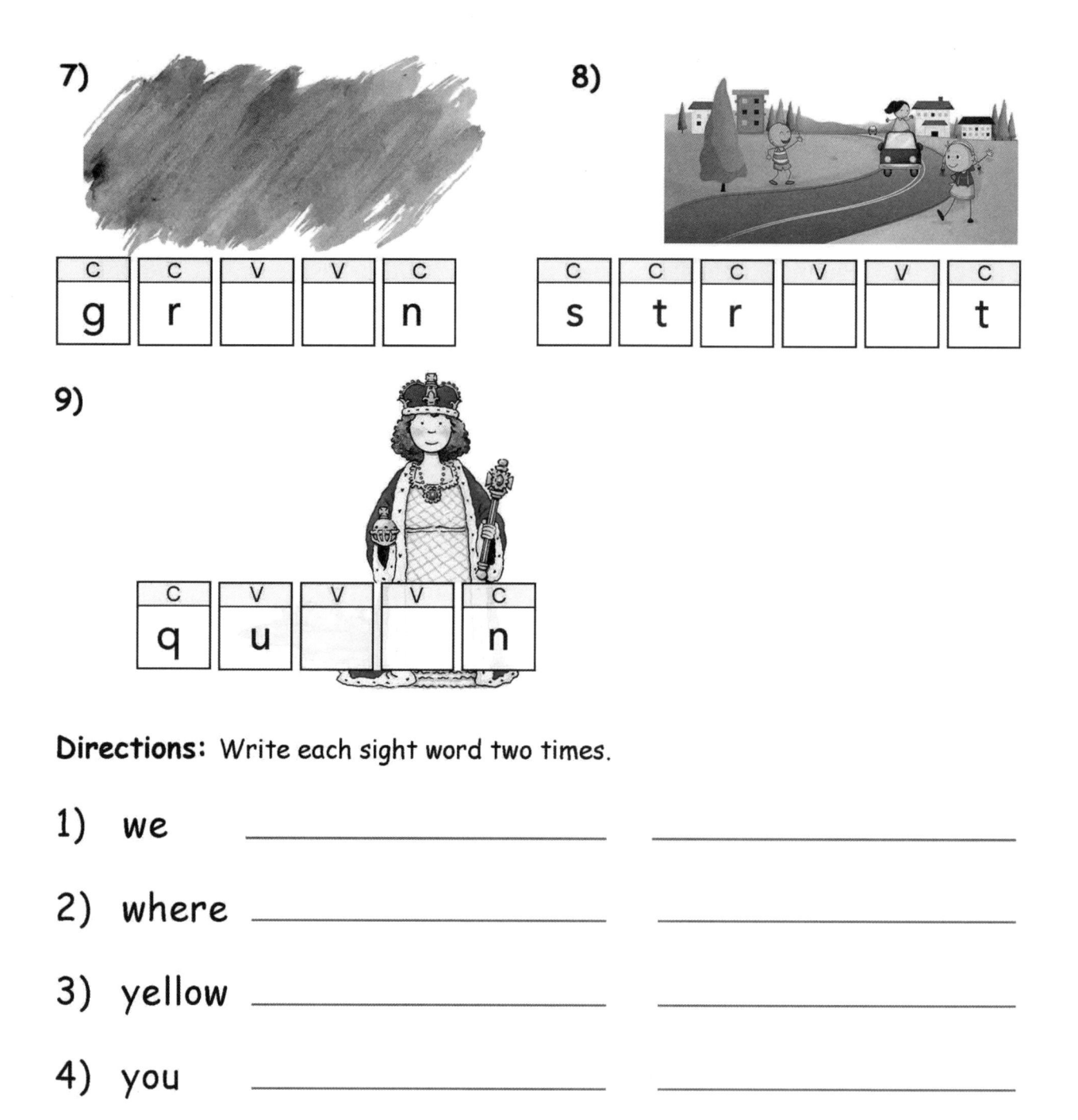

C	C	V	V	C
g	r			n

8)

C	C	C	V	V	C
s	t	r			t

9)

C	V	V	V	C
q	u			n

Directions: Write each sight word two times.

1) we _____   _____

2) where _____   _____

3) yellow _____   _____

4) you _____   _____

5) all _____   _____

6) am _____   _____

7) are _____   _____

Continue on following page.

8) at _____ _____

9) ate _____ _____

10) be _____ _____

11) black _____ _____

4.4 - Fables

Grammar Worksheet 2

Name _____.

Conjunctions

Directions:
Combine the **simple sentences** below into one **compound sentence** using the conjunction beside it.

Example:

I like playing outside. I don't like bugs. (but)

I like playing outside, <u>but</u> I don't like bugs.

1. I rode my bike down the street. My sister came too. (and)

2. I wanted to play outside after dinner. It was too dark out. (but)

3. My friend has a pool. We went swimming. (so)

Continue on the next page.

64

4. My mom said I could go to the pool. I could go to the park instead. (or)

5. I rolled down the hill. I didn't get muddy. (but)

Writing Checklist

Name _____.

Retell Checklist

Directions: Reread your writing carefully. Put a check in each box under **Author** as you complete each item. Once all the boxes are checked, give this to your teacher for the final edit.

Revise and Edit for the following:	Author	Teacher

1. Clarity and Meaning
   Ask yourself,
   "Will this retelling make sense to someone who hasn't read the full story?"
   "Did I include the characters, setting, and enough plot details to retell the story?"
   Rewrite parts that need revision.		

Revise and Edit for the following:	Author	Teacher

2. Correct Use of Words
   Ask yourself,
   "Did I use specific details and words?"
   "Did I explain?"
   "Do my sentences sound good together?"
   Rewrite parts that need revision.		

Revise and Edit for the following:	Author	Teacher

3. Capitalization
   Use capitals at the beginning of each sentence and for every name.
   Make corrections if needed.		

Continue on next page.

Revise and Edit for the following:	Author	Teacher

4. **Punctuation**
    Use periods, exclamation points, and question marks.
    Use quotation marks for dialogue.
    Make corrections if needed.		

Revise and Edit for the following:	Author	Teacher

5. **Spelling**
    Check for correct spelling.
    Make corrections if needed.		

4.4 - Fables

Handwriting Practice 2

Name _____.

Directions:
Write each letter across the line.

Example

u   u   u   u   u   u   u   u

u

u

y

y

i

i

j

j

4.4 - Fables

Name _____ .

Spelling Test

Directions:
As your teacher reads your words, write each spelling word on the blanks below.

Spelling Test

1) _____

2) _____

3) _____

4) _____

5) _____

6) _____

7) _____

8) _____

9) _____

10) _____

11) _____

12) _____

13) _____

14) _____

15) _____

16) _____

17) _____

18) _____

19) _____

20) _____

4.5 - Fables

Name _____.

Independent Reading

Independent Reading

Directions: Read your independent reading book for 30 minutes. When you are done, choose one of the main characters from the book and explain one of that character's traits.

I read _____ by _____
(book title) (author)

for 30 minutes today.

_____ _____
My Signature   Parent/Guardian Signature

Main Character's Name: _____   **Details**

Character Trait: _____

Write a short retelling of what happened in your story today. Remember to include the setting, characters, and events that took place.

_____
_____
_____
_____
_____

70   4.5 - Fables

Name _____ .

Journal Entry

Directions: Write your response to the prompt on the lines below. Don't forget to check for complete sentences as you write.

Prompt: What would you do if you had the power to turn everything you touched to gold? What would your life be like?

5.1 - Myths

Name _____

Spelling Worksheet

Rainbow Words

Directions:
Please choose three different colored pencils. Write each spelling word three times using each color.

brown _____ _____ _____

but _____ _____ _____

came _____ _____ _____

did _____ _____ _____

do _____ _____ _____

eat _____ _____ _____

four _____ _____ _____

get _____ _____ _____

good _____ _____ _____

have _____ _____ _____

he _____ _____ _____

into _____ _____ _____

Continue on the next page.

boil _____ _____ _____

boy _____ _____ _____

joy _____ _____ _____

toy _____ _____ _____

soil _____ _____ _____

foil _____ _____ _____

join _____ _____ _____

coin _____ _____ _____

5.2 - Myths

Name: _____.

Writing Graphic Organizer - Myths

Directions: Write the person you chose to write your character description about on the line below. Then, write his or her three traits and at least one reason why he or she has each trait.

Character Description Prewrite

Person: _____

Trait #1: _____

Details
- Reason #1:

- Reason #2:

Trait #2: _____

Details
- Reason #1:

- Reason #2:

Trait #3: _____

Details
- Reason #1:

- Reason #2:

5.2 - Myths

Handwriting Practice

Name _____.

Directions:
Use the dotted lines to help you write each letter on the first line. Continue writing each letter on your own on the second line.

Example

k k k k k k k k

k

Example

r r r r r r r r

r

Example

s s s s s s s s

s

5.2 - Myths

75

Name _____

Vocabulary Worksheet

Directions:
Use the word bank to fill in the blanks in the paragraph below.

WORD BANK:
treasure   wealthy
satisfy   astonished
frenzy   despair

The pirates were getting closer now. Their long journey was coming to an end. They had been at sea for ten long months in search of _____ that was said to be so large, that there would be more than enough for everyone on board. With all that gold, they would all be _____ for sure. They rowed to shore and pulled out their map. They followed it carefully and started digging. They were _____ to find that the treasure wasn't there. Had they read the map incorrectly? Yes, the map was smudged. What they thought read 20 paces was actually 30 paces. They walked 10 more steps. It was a _____ of activity as the pirates dug the hole again. Their shovels hit something hard. It was the treasure chest! They lifted the chest from the ground and pried it open. The pirates were filled with _____ . The chest was empty! Their map lead them to an empty treasure chest.

5.3 - Myths

Name _____

Fill in the Blanks: oi and oy

Spelling Worksheet

Directions: Fill in the blanks to spell each word with the **oi** or **oy** spelling.

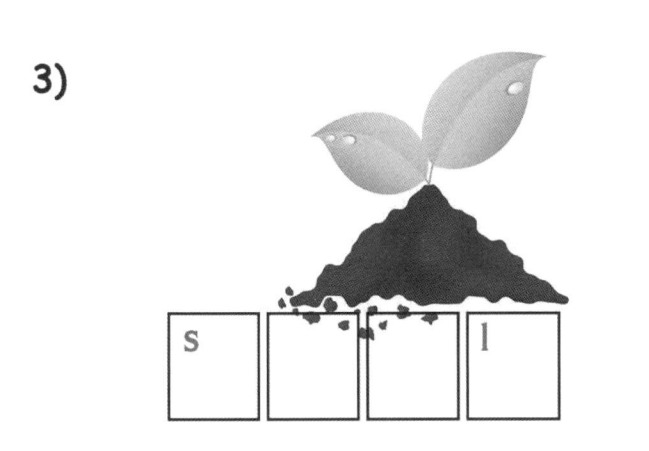

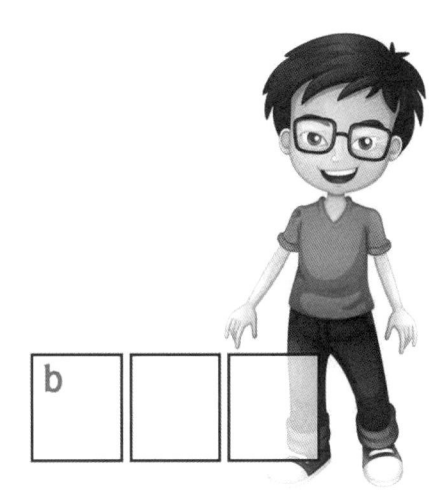

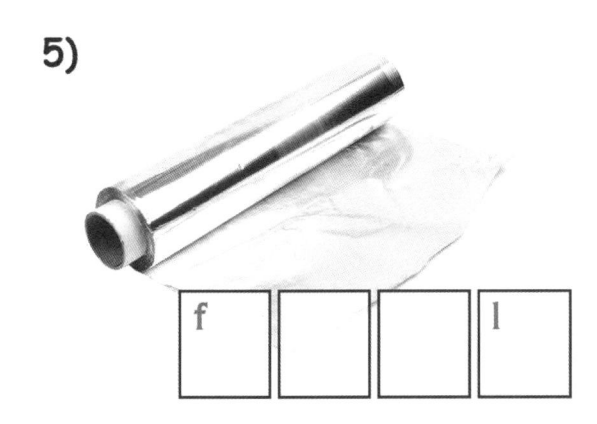

1) j ☐ ☐ ☐

2) b ☐ ☐ l

3) s ☐ ☐ l

4) b ☐ ☐

5) f ☐ ☐ l

6) t ☐ ☐

Continue on the following page.

5.4 - Myths

77

7) | j | | | n |

8) | c | | | n |

Directions: Write each sight word two times.

1) brown _____   _____

2) but   _____   _____

3) came _____   _____

4) did   _____   _____

5) do   _____   _____

6) eat   _____   _____

7) four _____   _____

8) get   _____   _____

9) good _____   _____

10) have _____   _____

11) he   _____   _____

12) into _____   _____

Grammar Worksheet

Name _____.

Common and Proper Nouns

Directions:
Write one **common noun** and one **proper noun** that appear in each sentence.

1. A great big oak tree is on the quarter for Connecticut.

   Common Noun: _____

   Proper Noun: _____

2. Georgia has a peach on its coin.

   Common Noun: _____

   Proper Noun: _____

3. Can you guess which quarter has the Statue of Liberty on it?

   Common Noun: _____

   Proper Noun: _____

4. Maine, the state my mom was born in, has a lighthouse on its quarter.

   Common Noun: _____

   Proper Noun: _____

Continue on the next page.

5.4 - Myths

Directions:
Find the error(s) with a common or proper noun in each sentence below and circle it.

1. Philadelphia is a large City in Pennsylvania.

2. We visited Central park in New York City last year.

3. I really want to visit Florida with my mom so we can go to disney world.

4. Have you ever traveled outside of your own State where you live?

5.4 Writing Checklist

Name _____

Character Description Checklist

Directions: Reread your writing carefully. Put a check in each box under **Author** as you complete each item. Once all the boxes are checked, submit your work to your **teacher** for the final check.

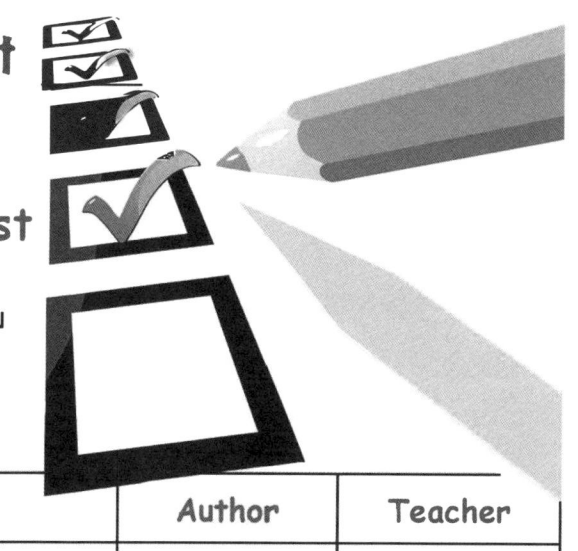

Revise and Edit for the following:	Author	Teacher
1. Clarity and Meaning **Ask yourself,** "Will this description make sense to someone who hasn't met this person?" "Did I include the three traits that describe this person?" Rewrite parts that need revision.		

Revise and Edit for the following:	Author	Teacher
2. Correct Use of Words **Ask yourself,** "Are specific details and words used?" "Did I explain the traits?" "Do the sentences sound good together?"" Rewrite parts that need revision.		

Revise and Edit for the following:	Author	Teacher
3. Capitalization Use capitals at the beginning of each sentence and for every name. Make corrections if needed.		

Continue on the next page.

5.4 - Myths

Revise and Edit for the following:	Author	Teacher
4. Punctuation Use periods, exclamation points, and question marks. Use quotation marks for dialogue. Make corrections if needed.		

Revise and Edit for the following:	Author	Teacher
5. Spelling Check for correct spelling. Make corrections if needed.		

Handwriting Practice

Name _____.

Directions:
Use the lines to help write each letter on the first line and continue writing each letter on your own on the next lines.

Example

k k k k k k k k

k

k

r

r

s

s

5.4 - Myths

83

Name _____

Spelling Test

Directions: As your teacher reads your words, write each spelling word on the blanks below.

1) _____   11) _____

2) _____   12) _____

3) _____   13) _____

4) _____   14) _____

5) _____   15) _____

6) _____   16) _____

7) _____   17) _____

8) _____   18) _____

9) _____   19) _____

10) _____ 20) _____

21) _____

5.5 - Myths

Name _____.

Independent Reading

Directions: Read your independent reading book for 30 minutes. When you are done, choose one of the main characters from the book and explain one of their character's traits.

I read _____ by _____
       (book title)   (author)

for 30 minutes today.

_____   _____
My Signature   Parent/Guardian Signature

Main Character's Name: _____   **Details**

Character Trait: _____

Why does that character have this character trait? Use details from the story to explain your answer.

_____
_____
_____
_____
_____
_____

5.5 - Myths

Name _____.

Journal Entry - *Why Tales*

Directions: Write your response to the prompt on the lines below. Don't forget to check for complete sentences as you write.

Prompt: What is something that you do really well? Explain why you think you do it so well.

6.1 - Why Tales

Name _____

Spelling - *Why Tales*

Rainbow Words

Directions:
Please choose three different colored pencils. Write each spelling word three times using each color.

like _____   _____   _____

must _____   _____   _____

new _____   _____   _____

no _____   _____   _____

now _____   _____   _____

on _____   _____   _____

our _____   _____   _____

out _____   _____   _____

please _____   _____   _____

pretty _____   _____   _____

ran _____   _____   _____

ride _____   _____   _____

Continue on the next page.

took _____ _____ _____

book _____ _____ _____

foot _____ _____ _____

good _____ _____ _____

loud _____ _____ _____

shout _____ _____ _____

cloud _____ _____ _____

Name _____.

Prewrite- *Why Tales*

Directions: Answer the questions below to help you plan your **why tale**.

1. What animal is your main character? Is it male or female?

_____
_____
_____

2. What is it that you are explaining?
   (Remember, why tales often start with "how or "why.")

_____
_____
_____

3. What other characters are there?

_____
_____
_____

Continue on following page.

6.2 - Why Tales

4. Where and when do they live?

_____

- -

_____

- -

_____

5. What is the problem in your story that leads to the thing you are explaining?

_____

- -

_____

- -

_____

6. How is the problem solved?

_____

- -

_____

- -

_____

Handwriting Practice 1

Name _____.

Handwriting - Why Tales

Directions:
Use the grey lines to help you write each letter on the first line. Continue writing each letter on your own on the following lines.

Example

o o o o o o o o

o

o

Example

w w w w w w w

w

w

6.2 - Why Tales

Name _____.

Vocabulary - *Why Tales*

Directions:
Use the word bank to fill in the blanks in the sentences below.

6.3 Vocabulary Worksheet

WORD BANK:
lazy   desert   yoke   plow
magic   reflection

1. The farmer put the _____ around the oxen's neck to prepare them for work.

2. She used _____ to make the rabbit disappear before their eyes.

3. The _____ dog slept in the sun all day long.

4. The farmer had to _____ the fields to get them ready for planting.

5. He saw his messy hair in his _____ in the mirror.

6. He rode his camel through the hot, dry _____ to reach the next town.

92

6.3 - Why Tales

6.3 Reading Graphic Organizer

Name _____.

How the Camel Got His Hump

Directions: As you read the story, write down the main idea and three details to support it.

Main Idea: _____

Detail: _____

Detail: _____

Detail: _____

6.3 - Why Tales

6.4 Spelling Worksheet

Name _____.

Fill in the Blanks - *Why Tales*

Directions: Fill in the blanks to spell each word using **oo** or **ou**.

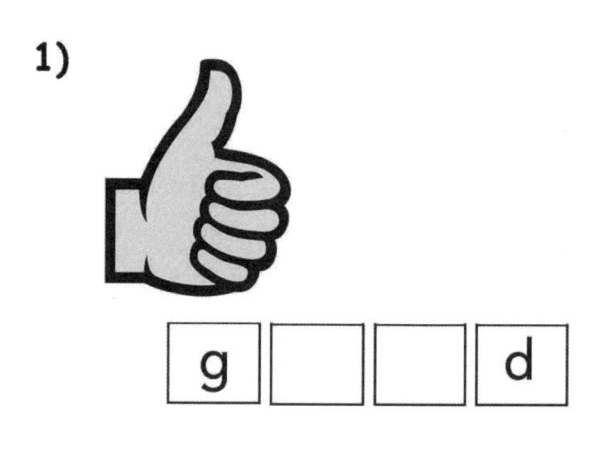

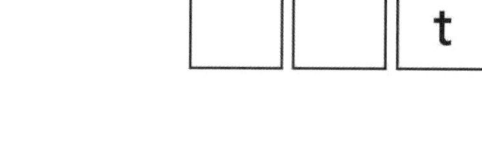

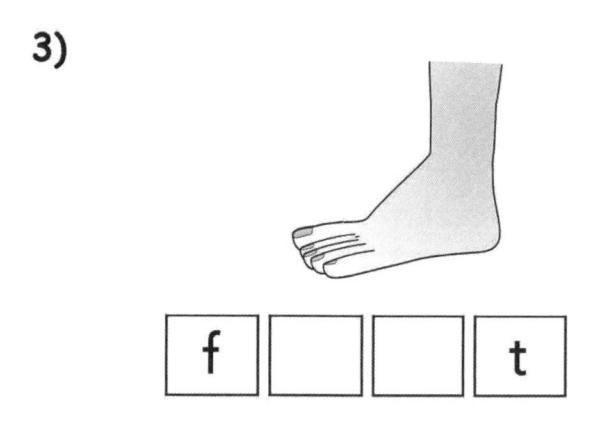

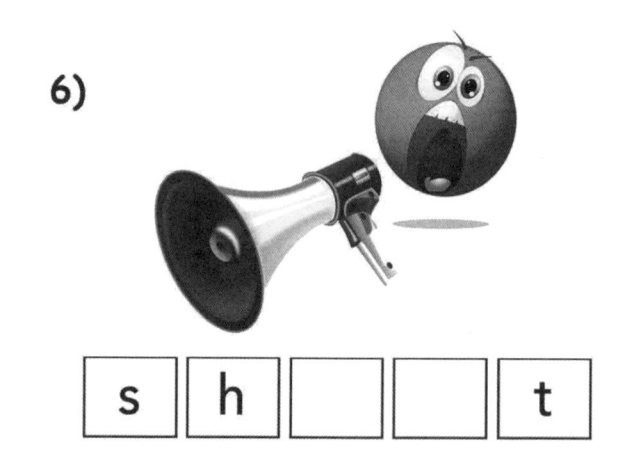

1) g [ ] [ ] d

2) [ ] [ ] t

3) f [ ] [ ] t

4) c l [ ] [ ] d

5) b [ ] [ ] k

6) s h [ ] [ ] t

Continue on following page.

94 6.4 - Why Tales

7) l ☐ ☐ d

8) t ☐ ☐ k

Directions: Circle the correct spelling of the word and then write the correct spelling on the blank.

Circle Correct Spelling   Write Correct Word

1. like   leke   lik   _____

2. muste   must   moust   _____

3. new   nu   nuw   _____

4. noo   nou   no   _____

5. now   nou   nuw   _____

6. onn   on   un   _____

7. owr   oure   our   _____

8. out   oute   owt   _____

9. plese   please   pleese   _____

10. prety   pretty   pretti   _____

11. ran   rane   raan   _____

12. ridd   ried   ride   _____

6.4 - Why Tales

6.4 Grammar Worksheet

Name _____.

Nouns - *Why Tales*

Directions: Write one **singular noun** and one **plural noun** that appear in each sentence.

1. Trees line the street that leads to the farm.

    Singular Noun: _____

    Plural Noun: _____

2. The farmer cares for lots of different animals.

    Singular Noun: _____

    Plural Noun: _____

3. At the farm, I counted five ponies.

    Singular Noun: _____

    Plural Noun: _____

4. The chickens were laying eggs in the barn.

    Singular Noun: _____

    Plural Noun: _____

Continue on the next page.

Directions: Find the error with a **plural noun** in each sentence below and circle it. Rewrite the plural noun correctly on the line.

1. There were other familys visiting the farm that day.

   Correction: _____

2. They were handing out old loafs of bread to feed the ducks.

   Correction: _____

3. We saw the sheeps being herded by a sheepdog.

   Correction: _____

4. There were so many childs there having a great time in the petting zoo.

   Correction: _____

6.4 - Why Tales

6.4 Writing Checklist

Name _____.

Why Tale Checklist

Directions: Reread your writing carefully. Put a check in each box under **Author** as you complete each item. Once all the boxes are checked, your **peer partner** will check your paragraph and put a check in each box.

Revise and Edit for the following:	Author	Peer Partner
1. Clarity and Meaning *Ask yourself,* "Does the why tale tell a how or why story about an animal?" "Is the problem of the story clear?" Rewrite parts that need revision.		

Revise and Edit for the following:	Author	Peer Partner
2. Correct Use of Words *Ask yourself,* "Are specific details and words used?" "Are explanations used when needed?" "Do the sentences sound good together?"" Rewrite parts that need revision.		

Revise and Edit for the following:	Author	Peer Partner
3. Capitalization Use capitals at the beginning of each sentence and for every name. Make corrections if needed.		

Continue on the next page.

Revise and Edit for the following:	Author	Teacher

4. Punctuation
    Use periods, exclamation points, and question marks.
    Use quotation marks for dialogue.
    Make corrections if needed.		

Revise and Edit for the following:	Author	Teacher

5. Spelling
    Check for correct spelling.
    Make corrections if needed.		

Name _____.

Handwriting - *Why Tales*

Handwriting Practice 2

Directions:
Write each letter across the line.

Example

o   o   o   o   o   o   o   o

o

o

o

w

w

w

100

6.4 - Why Tales

Name _____.

Spelling Test - *Why Tales*

Directions:
As your teacher reads your words, write each spelling word on the blanks below.

Spelling Test

1) _____
2) _____
3) _____
4) _____
5) _____
6) _____
7) _____
8) _____
9) _____
10) _____

11) _____
12) _____
13) _____
14) _____
15) _____
16) _____
17) _____
18) _____
19) _____
20) _____

Independent Reading

Name _____.

Independent Reading - *Why Tales*

Directions: Read your independent reading book for 30 minutes. When you are done, write a short summary of what you have read.

I read _____ by _____
          (book title)   (author)

for 30 minutes today.

_____   _____
         My Signature   Parent/Guardian Signature

Write a short summary about what you read today.

_____ Details
_____
_____
_____
_____
_____
_____
_____

6.5 - Why Tales

Name _____.

Journal Entry - *Solving Problems*

Directions: Write your response to the prompt on the lines below. Don't forget to check for complete sentences as you write.

Prompt: Describe a time when you solved a problem. What was the problem and how did you solve it?

_____
_____
_____
_____
_____
_____
_____
_____
_____
_____
_____
_____
_____
_____
_____
_____

7.1 - Solving Problems

Name _____.

Spelling - *Solving Problems*

Rainbow Words

Directions:
Please choose three different colored pencils. Write each spelling word three times using each color.

saw _____ _____ _____

say _____ _____ _____

she _____ _____ _____

so _____ _____ _____

soon _____ _____ _____

that _____ _____ _____

there _____ _____ _____

they _____ _____ _____

this _____ _____ _____

too _____ _____ _____

under _____ _____ _____

want _____ _____ _____

Continue on the next page.

high _____ _____ _____

right _____ _____ _____

fight _____ _____ _____

sight _____ _____ _____

sky _____ _____ _____

by _____ _____ _____

my _____ _____ _____

cry _____ _____ _____

7.2 - Solving Problems

Handwriting Practice 1

Name _____.

Handwriting - *Solving Problems*

Directions:
Use the grey lines to help you write each letter on the first line. Continue writing each letter on your own on the following lines.

Example

Example

106   7.2 - Solving Problems

7.4 Spelling Worksheet

Name _____.

Spelling - *Solving Problems*

Directions:
Write each of the spelling words below. Use a **red colored pencil** to write the consonants and a **blue colored pencil** to write the vowels.

Example:
fly   fly

1) high _____

2) right _____

3) fight _____

4) sight _____

5) sky _____

6) by _____

7) my _____

8) cry _____

Continue on the next page.

7.4 - Solving Problems

Directions: Circle the correct spelling of the word and then write the correct spelling on the blank.

soon

Circle Correct Spelling			Write Correct Word

1. saw   sawe   sau   _____

2. sae   say   sai   _____

3. she   shee   shi   _____

4. soo   sou   so   _____

5. sune   soon   soun   _____

6. tat   that   thit   _____

7. there   tere   theur   _____

8. thei   they   thy   _____

9. thise   tis   this   _____

10. too   tuo   tuu   _____

11. under   undur   undir   _____

12. wnt   wunt   want   _____

7.4 - Solving Problems

Name _____.

Vocabulary - *Solving Problems*

Directions:
Use the word bank to fill in the blanks in the sentences below.

7.4 Vocabulary Worksheet

WORD BANK:
harsh   capture   doze
outcome   starve   risk

1. I love to _____ in the hammock on warm, sunny days.

2. My mom tried to _____ the mouse in our kitchen, but he escaped.

3. The stray dog looked like he hadn't eaten in days and might _____.

4. The sun was very _____, so I put on my sunglasses.

5. She took a _____ by trying a new cake recipe, but it turned out great!

6. He didn't like the _____ of the game because he lost.

7.4 - Solving Problems   109

Name _____.

Reading - *Solving Problems*

7.4 Reading Worksheet

Sassy, Not Sissy

Saving the Manatees

Directions:
Please answer the questions below after reading "**Sassy, Not Sissy**" and "**Saving the Manatees.**"

1. What is the problem in "Sassy, Not Sissy?"
   _____
   _____
   _____
   _____
   _____
   _____

2. How was the problem solved?
   _____
   _____
   _____
   _____
   _____
   _____

Continue on the next page.

110 7.4 - Solving Problems

3. What is the problem in "Saving the Manatees?"

_____
_____
_____
_____
_____
_____
_____

4. How can we work to solve the manatee problem?

_____
_____
_____
_____
_____
_____
_____

7.4 - Solving Problems

7.4 Grammar Worksheet

Name _____.

Grammar - Solving Problems

Directions:
Circle the **concrete nouns** and underline the **abstract nouns** in the sentence below.

1. He has a lot of confidence when it comes to his soccer skills.

2. It was a surprise when her friends jumped out at her party.

3. The clown used humor to make the children laugh.

4. Happiness means different things to different people.

5. She takes a lot of pride in her artwork.

6. The monkeys at the zoo have a lot of curiosity.

Handwriting Practice 2

Name _____

Handwriting - *Solving Problems*

Directions:
Use the grey lines to help you write each letter on the first line. Continue writing each letter on your own on the following lines.

Example

b b b b b b b b

b

b

b

v

v

v

7.4 - Solving Problems 113

Name _____

Spelling Test

Spelling - *Solving Problems*

Directions:
As your teacher reads your words, write each spelling word on the blanks below.

1) _____   11) _____

2) _____   12) _____

3) _____   13) _____

4) _____   14) _____

5) _____   15) _____

6) _____   16) _____

7) _____   17) _____

8) _____   18) _____

9) _____   19) _____

10) _____   20) _____

7.5 - Solving Problems

Name _____.

7.5 Reading Worksheet

Literal and Nonliteral - *Solving Problems*

Directions: Complete the worksheet using what you know about **literal** and **nonliteral** meanings.

Reading

Literal Meaning

Definition: Words denote what they really mean

Explanation of Literal Meaning: (your own)

_____

_____

_____

Example: Spill the beans

Illustration of Literal Meaning:

Continue on following page.

7.5 - Solving Problems

115

Nonliteral Meaning

Definition: Words mean something else than what they mean

Explanation of Nonliteral Meaning: (your own)

_____

_____

_____

Example:

Spill the beans

Illustration of Nonliteral Meaning:

7.5 - Solving Problems

7.5 Writing Worksheet

Name _____.

Writing - *Solving Problems*

Directions:
Read the following list of writing ideas.
Create a topic sentence for each.

1. My favorite amusement park ride

   Topic Sentence: _____

   _____

   _____

2. The surprise party

   Topic Sentence: _____

   _____

   _____

3. When the wheel came off my bike

   Topic Sentence: _____

   _____

   _____

4. When my baby sister was born

   Topic Sentence: _____

   _____

   _____

7.5 - Solving Problems

7.5 Independent Reading

Name _____

Reading - *Solving Problems*

Directions: Read your independent reading book for 30 minutes. When you are done, write a short summary of what you have read.

I read _____ by _____
         (book title)   (author)

for 30 minutes today.

_____   _____
     My Signature   Parent/Guardian Signature

Write a short summary about what you read today.   **Details**

_____
_____
_____
_____
_____
_____
_____

118   7.5 - Solving Problems

Name _____.

Journal Entry - *Asking Questions*

Directions: Write your response to the prompt on the lines below. Don't forget to check for complete sentences as you write.

Prompt: What is your favorite book? Why?

8.1 - Asking Questions

Name _____.

Spelling - Asking Questions

8.2 Spelling Worksheet

Rainbow Words

Directions:
Please choose three different colored pencils. Write each spelling word three times using each color.

was _____ _____ _____

well _____ _____ _____

went _____ _____ _____

what _____ _____ _____

white _____ _____ _____

who _____ _____ _____

will _____ _____ _____

with _____ _____ _____

yes _____ _____ _____

after _____ _____ _____

again _____ _____ _____

an _____ _____ _____

Continue on the next page.

telescope _____ _____ _____

history _____ _____ _____

monster _____ _____ _____

crystal _____ _____ _____

rescue _____ _____ _____

discover _____ _____ _____

Name _____.

Writing Graphic Organizer -
Asking Questions

Opinion Paragraph Prewrite

Directions:
What is something that you or your family needs? Write your opinion on the line below. Then, list at least two reasons with details.

Opinion: _____

Reason #1: _____

Details

Reason #2: _____

Details

Reason #3: _____

Details

122   8.2 - Asking Questions

Handwriting Practice 1

Name _____.

Handwriting - Asking Questions

Directions:
Use the grey lines to help you write each letter on the first line. Continue writing each letter on your own on the following lines.

Example

Example

8.2 - Asking Questions

Name _____

Vocabulary Word Crossword -
Asking Questions

Directions: Use the definitions to complete the crossword puzzle using your vocabulary words.

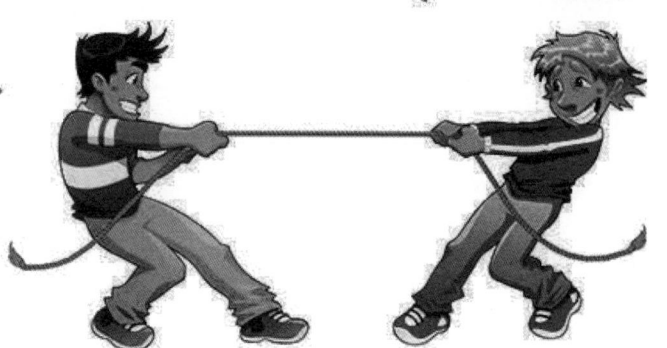

8.3 Vocabulary Worksheet

Across:
2. easily torn or hurt
3. to draw in a breath sharply
4. to offer oneself for a service
5. to declare in advance

Down:
1. made a great effort to overcome something or someone
2. a drawing, sketch, plan or chart that makes something clearer or easier to understand

8.3 - Asking Questions

Spelling Worksheet

Name _____.

Fill in the Blanks - *Asking Questions*

Directions: Fill in the blanks to spell each word.

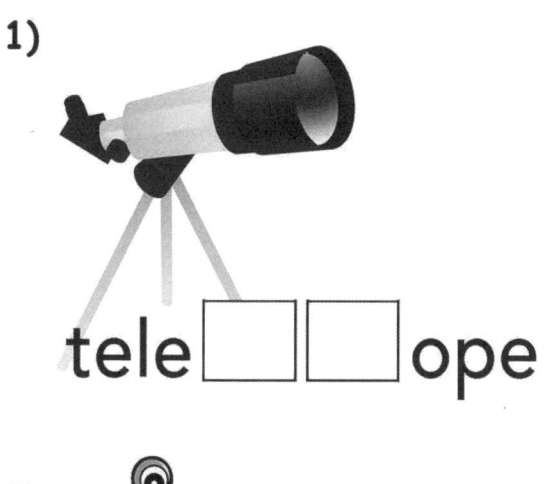

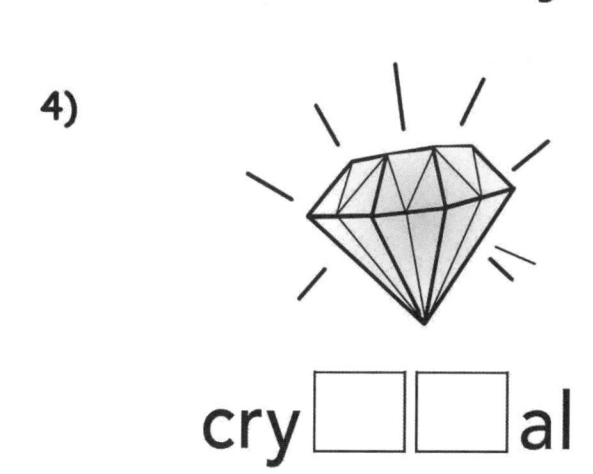

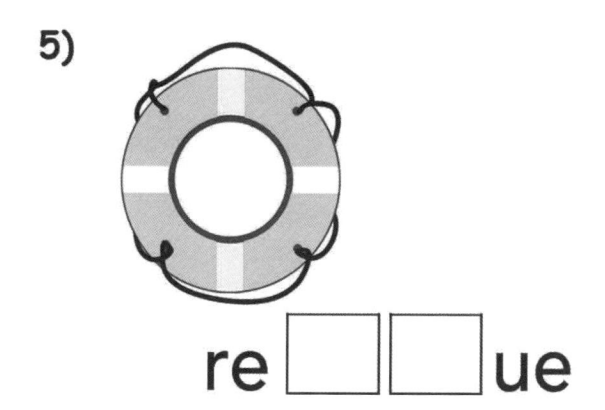

1) tele☐☐ope

2) hi☐☐ory

3) mon☐☐er

4) cry☐☐al

5) re☐☐ue

6) di☐☐over

Continue on following page.

8.4 - Asking Questions

Directions: Circle the correct spelling of the word and then write the correct spelling on the blank.

Circle Correct Spelling   Write Correct Word

1. wus   was   wuse   _____

2. well   wel   wele   _____

3. went   wentt   wint   _____

4. whut   wat   what   _____

5. white   wite   whit   _____

6. whoo   whu   who   _____

7. will   wil   wile   _____

8. withe   with   wite   _____

9. yes   yus   yse   _____

10. aftre   after   aftur   _____

11. agan   agane   again   _____

12. ann   ane   an   _____

8.4 - Asking Questions

Name _____

8.4 Reading Worksheet

Our Class Eggs

Reading - *Asking Questions*

Directions:
Please answer the question below after reading "**Our Class Eggs**". Circle the correct answer.

1. Because the mother hen can't sit on her eggs, what did they bring to the classroom?
    a. incubator
    b. elevator
    c. fake hen

2. What was one of the responsibilities of the students?
    a. help the chicks out of their shells
    b. turn the eggs three times a day
    c. bring the eggs home each night

3. What happened to the last egg?
    a. it didn't hatch
    b. it fell on the floor
    c. it hatched the biggest chick

4. What did the class learn from having the eggs in the classroom?

_____
_____
_____
_____
_____

8.4 - Asking Questions   127

8.4 Grammar Worksheet

Name _____.

Verb Types - Asking Questions

Directions:
Identify the type of verb underlined in each sentence below. Write whether it is an **action verb**, **linking verb**, or **helping verb** on the line.

1. Sara and I <u>walked</u> to our friend's house after school.

    Type of Verb: _____

2. Walking the dog <u>is</u> my favorite chore.

    Type of Verb: _____

3. He <u>ran</u> as fast as he could to first base.

    Type of Verb: _____

4. Dr. Green <u>has</u> driven to the hospital every day.

    Type of Verb: _____

5. My dad takes us <u>hiking</u> every Saturday.

    Type of Verb: _____

6. The baker <u>bakes</u> great cakes.

    Type of Verb: _____

Directions: Write three sentences below with at least one verb in each. Circle the verb or verbs in each sentence.

1. _____

2. _____

3. _____

8.4 Writing Checklist

Name _____

Opinion Paragraph Checklist

Directions: Reread your writing carefully. Put a check in each box under **Author** as you complete each item. Once all the boxes are checked, your **peer partner** will check your paragraph and put a check in each box.

Revise and Edit for the following:	Author	Peer Partner
1. Clarity and Meaning 　**Ask yourself,** 　"Does the paragraph explain why you want something for yourself or your family?" 　"Are the reasons clear?" 　Rewrite parts that need revision.		

Revise and Edit for the following:	Author	Peer Partner
2. Correct Use of Words 　**Ask yourself,** 　"Are specific details and words used?" 　"Are explanations used when needed?" 　"Do the sentences sound good together?"" 　Rewrite parts that need revision.		

Revise and Edit for the following:	Author	Peer Partner
3. Capitalization 　Use capitals at the beginning of each sentence and for every name. 　Make corrections if needed.		

Continue on the next page.

Revise and Edit for the following:	Author	Peer Partner

4. Punctuation
 	
    Use periods, exclamation points, and question marks.
 	
    Use quotation marks for dialogue.
 	
    Make corrections if needed.		

Revise and Edit for the following:	Author	Peer Partner

5. Spelling
 	
    Check for correct spelling.
 	
    Make corrections if needed.		

Handwriting Practice 2

Name _____.

Handwriting - *Asking Questions*

Directions:
Write each letter across the line.

Example

m m m m m m m m

n

n

n

m

m

m

8.4 - Asking Questions

Name _____.

Spelling Test

Spelling - *Asking Questions*

Directions:
As your teacher reads your words, write each spelling word on the blanks below.

1) _____

2) _____

3) _____

4) _____

5) _____

6) _____

7) _____

8) _____

9) _____

10) _____

11) _____

12) _____

13) _____

14) _____

15) _____

16) _____

17) _____

18) _____

Name _____.

Sequence of Events

Directions:
Please answer the question below after reading "**Our Class Eggs**". Include all of the major events in sequence.

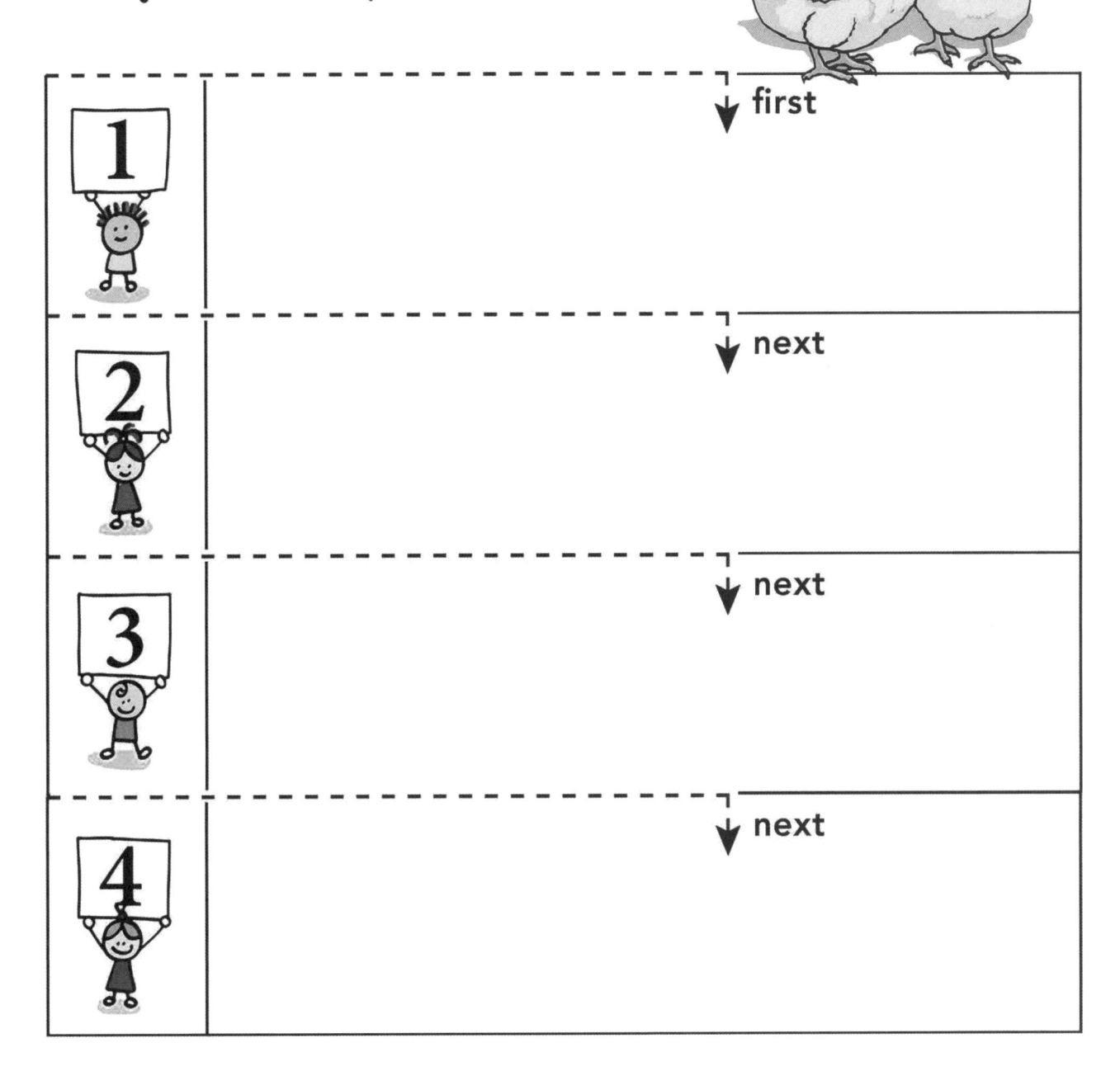

8.5 Reading Worksheet

Our Class Eggs

1	first
2	next
3	next
4	next

Continue on the following page.

8.5 - Asking Questions

133

next

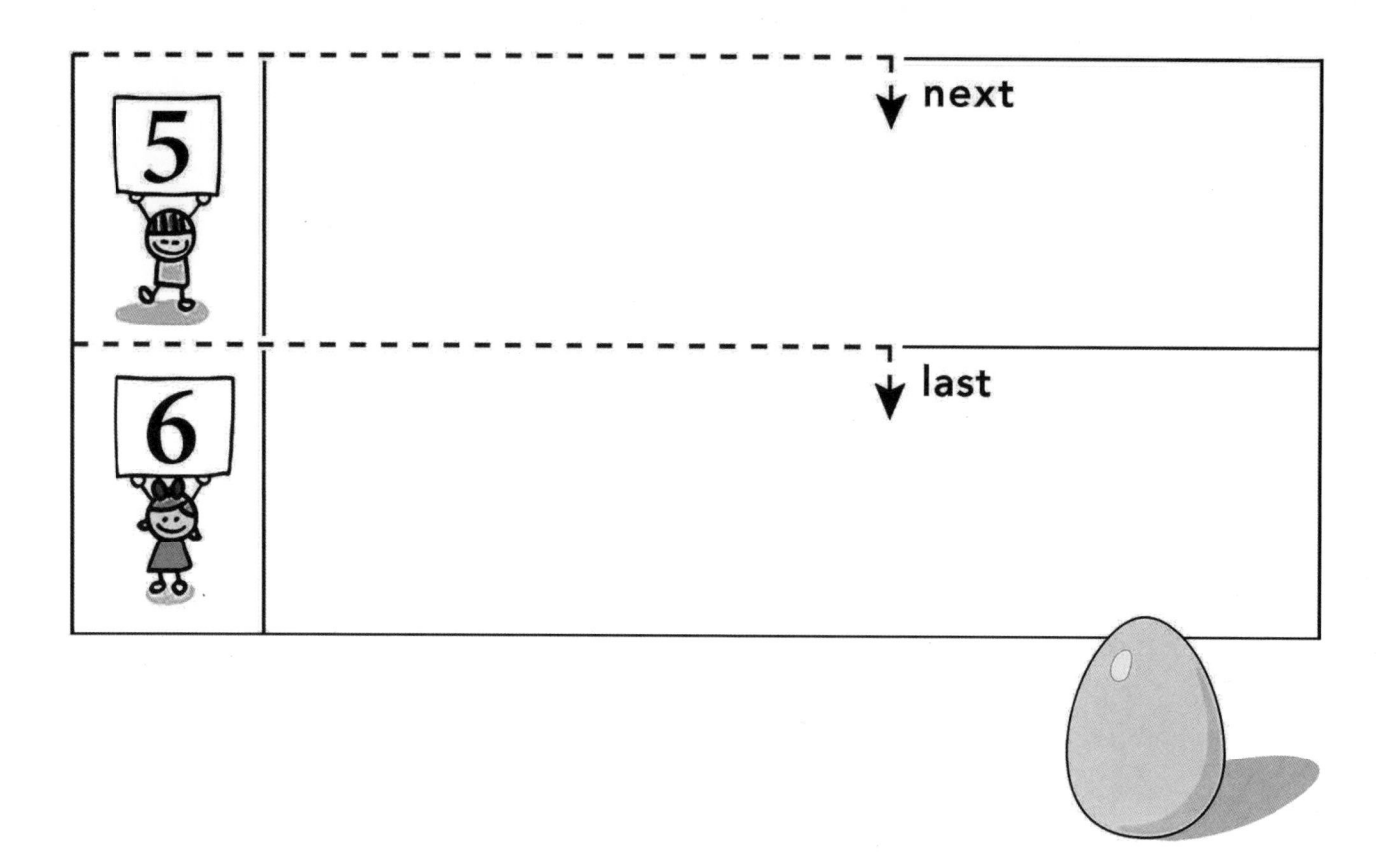

last

134 8.5 - Asking Questions

8.5 Independent Reading

Name _____.

Reading - *Asking Questions*

Reading

Directions: Read your independent reading book for 30 minutes. When you are done, list a sequence of the important events that you read today. Use as many of the boxes as you need.

I read _____ by _____
           (book title)   (author)

for 30 minutes today.

_____   _____
My Signature   Parent/Guardian Signature

List the sequence of the major events that you read today.

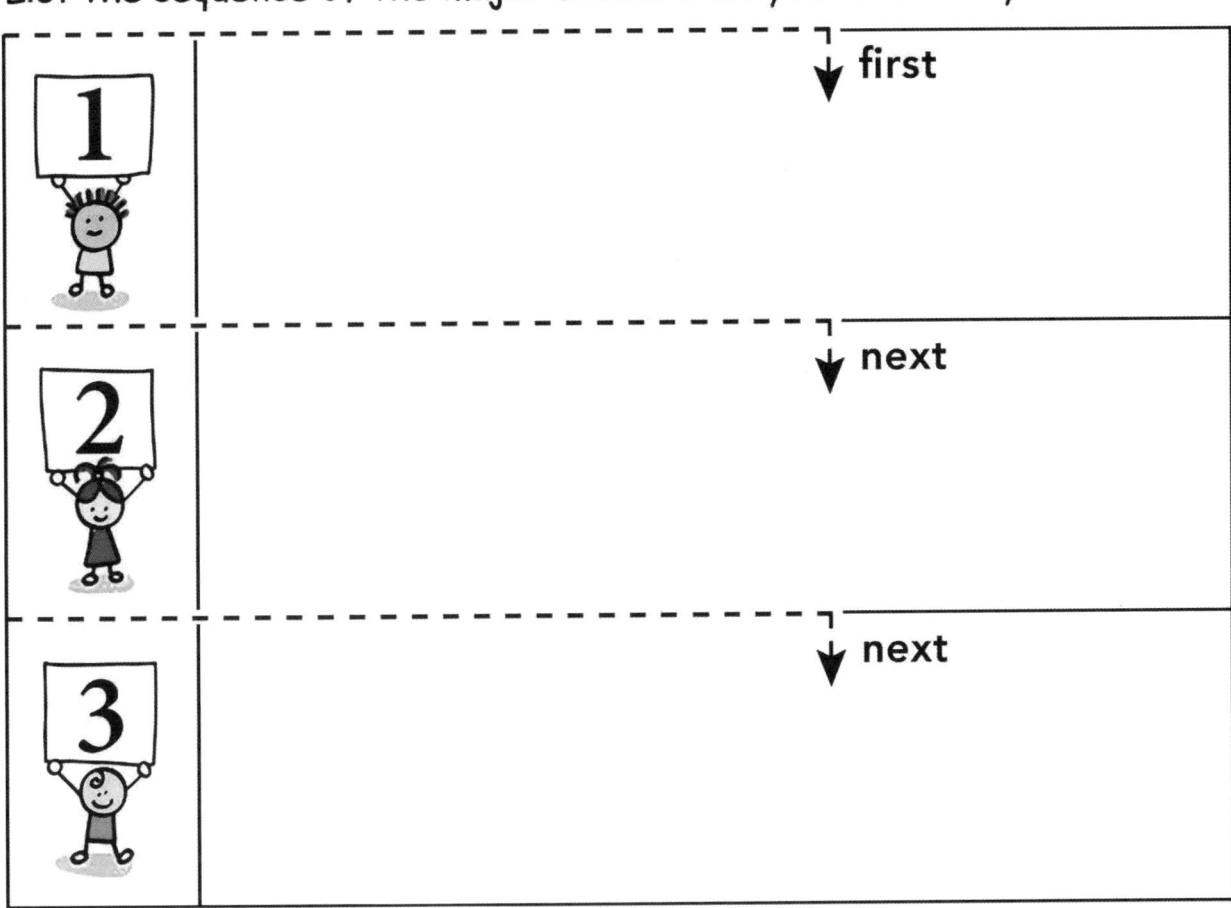

1	↓ **first**
2	↓ **next**
3	↓ **next**

Continue on the following page.

8.5 - Asking Questions   135

↓ next

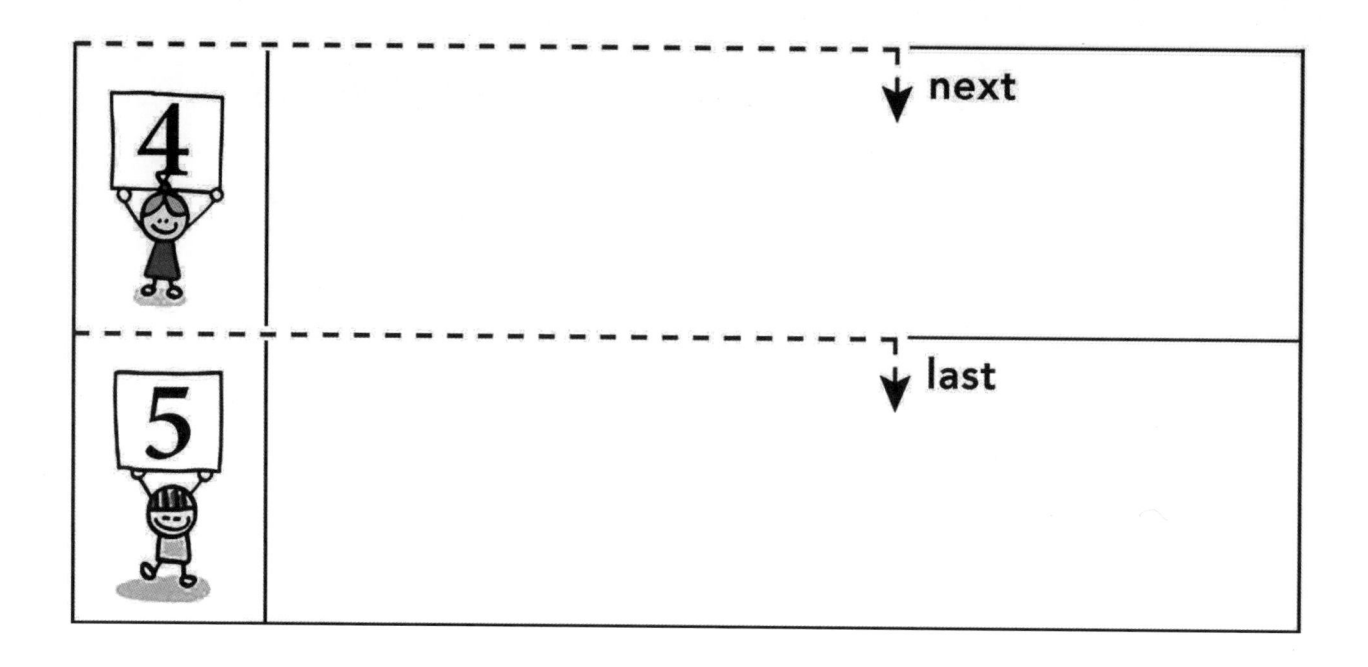

↓ last

Name _____.

Journal Entry - *Inventions*

Directions: Write your response to the prompt on the lines below. Don't forget to check for complete sentences as you write.

Prompt: If you could travel through time, which time period would you want to visit? Why?

9.1 - Inventions

Name _____

Spelling - *Inventions*

9.2 Spelling Worksheet

Rainbow Words

Directions:
Please choose three different colored pencils. Write each spelling word three times using each color.

any _____ _____ _____

as _____ _____ _____

ask _____ _____ _____

by _____ _____ _____

could _____ _____ _____

every _____ _____ _____

fly _____ _____ _____

from _____ _____ _____

give _____ _____ _____

going _____ _____ _____

had _____ _____ _____

has _____ _____ _____

Continue on the next page.

scrap   _____ _____ _____

splash _____ _____ _____

split   _____ _____ _____

spray   _____ _____ _____

spring _____ _____ _____

squeak _____ _____ _____

strap   _____ _____ _____

string _____ _____ _____

9.2 - Inventions

Name _____

Writing Graphic Organizer - Inventions

Opinion Paragraph Prewrite

Directions: Choose your topic from the choices below. You will need to write about how you disagree with one of these topics. **Circle your choice.** After you have picked your topic, list your reasons and explanations for your opinion below. You should have at least two reasons.

Choice 1: Your parents want to make bedtime earlier.

Choice 2: Your teacher wants to get rid of recess.

Choice 3: Your best friend wants you to have your birthday party at an ice rink.

Reason #1: _____

Details

Reason #2: _____

Details

Reason #3: _____

Details

Name _____.

Handwriting - *Inventions*

Directions:
Use the grey lines to help you write each letter on the first line. Continue writing each letter on your own on the following lines.

Handwriting Practice 1

Example

Example

Example

9.2 - Inventions

141

Name _____.

Vocabulary Word Crossword -
Inventions

Directions: Use the definitions to complete the crossword puzzle using your vocabulary words.

9.3 Vocabulary Worksheet

Across:

1. to take care of according to a routine
5. a way, plan or procedure for doing something
6. having a sharp mind

Down:

2. to be dependent
3. adapted to a use or purpose
4. quick in learning

Name _____.

9.4 Spelling Worksheet

Fill in the Blanks - *Inventions*

Directions: Fill in the blanks to spell each word.

1)  ☐☐☐ap

2) 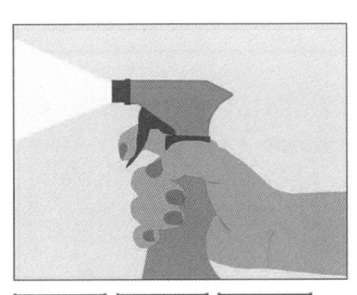 ☐☐☐ay

3) ☐☐☐eak

4)  ☐☐☐it

5)  ☐☐☐ing

6)  ☐☐☐ash

Continue on following page.

9.4 - Inventions

7) ☐☐☐ing

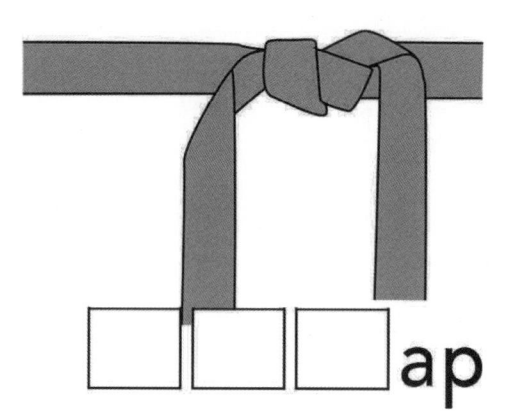

8) ☐☐☐ap

Directions: Circle the correct spelling of the word and then write the correct spelling on the blank.

Circle Correct Spelling			Write Correct Word
1. ani	ane	any	_____
2. as	az	azz	_____
3. ask	askk	azk	_____
4. bi	by	bie	_____
5. culd	coud	could	_____
6. every	evary	evry	_____
7. fli	flie	fly	_____
8. from	fromm	frum	_____
9. geve	give	giv	_____
10. goin	going	gong	_____
11. had	haad	haid	_____
12. hase	has	hse	_____

9.4 Grammar Worksheet

Name _____ .

Verbs - *Inventions*

Directions:
Fill in the blank using the correct past or present form of the verb in parentheses.

1. I _____ (run) home from school yesterday.

2. Did you just _____ (fall) from the monkey bars?

3. Carly didn't want to _____ (walk) home from the park in the rain.

4. Did you hear that he _____ (steal) that girl's ball at recess?

5. I _____ (win) first place!

6. She _____ (eat) three pieces of pie for dessert last night.

Directions: Write a sentence using the verb given. Circle whether you use the past or present tense.

1. jump   Past or Present

_____

2. lose   Past or Present

_____

3. shake   Past or Present

_____

9.4 - Inventions

9.4 Writing Checklist

Name _____.

Opinion Paragraph Checklist

Directions: Reread your writing carefully. Put a check in each box under **Author** as you complete each item. Once all the boxes are checked, submit your work to your **teacher** for the final check.

Revise and Edit for the following:	Author	Teacher
1. Clarity and Meaning *Ask yourself,* "Does the paragraph explain my opinion?" "Are the reasons and explanations clear?" Rewrite parts that need revision.		

Revise and Edit for the following:	Author	Teacher
2. Correct Use of Words *Ask yourself,* "Are specific details and words used?" "Are explanations used when needed?" "Do the sentences sound good together?"" Rewrite parts that need revision.		

Revise and Edit for the following:	Author	Teacher
3. Capitalization Use capitals at the beginning of each sentence and for every name. Make corrections if needed.		

Continue on the next page.

Revise and Edit for the following:	Author	Teacher

4. Punctuation
    Use periods, exclamation points, and question marks.
    Use quotation marks for dialogue.
    Make corrections if needed.		

Revise and Edit for the following:	Author	Teacher

5. Spelling
    Check for correct spelling.
    Make corrections if needed.		

Name _____.

Handwriting - *Inventions*

Directions:
Use the grey lines to help you write each letter on the first line. Continue writing each letter on your own on the following lines.

Handwriting Practice 2

Example

Name _____.

Spelling Test

Spelling - *Inventions*

Directions:
As your teacher reads your words, write each spelling word on the blanks below.

1) _____   11) _____

2) _____   12) _____

3) _____   13) _____

4) _____   14) _____

5) _____   15) _____

6) _____   16) _____

7) _____   17) _____

8) _____   18) _____

9) _____   19) _____

10) _____   20) _____

9.5 - Inventions

9.5 Independent Reading

Name _____

Reading - *Inventions*

Directions: Read your independent reading book for 30 minutes. When you are done, write a short summary of what you have read.

I read _____ by _____
              (book title)   (author)

for 30 minutes today.

_____   _____
My Signature   Parent/Guardian Signature

Write a short summary about what you read today.   **Details**

_____
_____
_____
_____
_____
_____
_____

Name _____ .

Journal Entry - *Pond Animals*

Directions: Write your response to the prompt on the lines below. Don't forget to check for complete sentences as you write.

Prompt: Describe what you would see and do during a day at the pond.

_____
_____
_____
_____
_____
_____
_____
_____
_____
_____
_____
_____
_____
_____
_____

10.1 - Pond Animals

Name _____.

Spelling - Pond Animals

10.2 Spelling Worksheet

Rainbow Words

Directions:
Please choose three different colored pencils. Write each spelling word three times using each color.

here   _____   _____   _____

him   _____   _____   _____

his   _____   _____   _____

how   _____   _____   _____

just   _____   _____   _____

know   _____   _____   _____

let   _____   _____   _____

live   _____   _____   _____

may   _____   _____   _____

of   _____   _____   _____

old   _____   _____   _____

once   _____   _____   _____

Continue on the next page.

10.2 - Pond Animals

three _____ _____ _____

thread _____ _____ _____

throne _____ _____ _____

throat _____ _____ _____

throb _____ _____ _____

thrill _____ _____ _____

10.2 - Pond Animals

Name _____.

Writing Graphic Organizer - *Pond Animals*

Compare and Contrast

Directions: Write your topic sentence on the line below. Then, list the similarities and differences between your two items. Finally, write your conclusion.

Paragraph Prewrite

Topic Sentence: _____

_____

Similarities

Details

Differences

Details

Conclusion: _____

_____

154

10.2 - Pond Animals

Handwriting Practice 1

Name _____.

Handwriting - Pond Animals

Directions:
Use the grey lines to help you write each letter on the first line. Continue writing each letter on your own on the following lines.

Example

a a a a a a a a

a

Example

c c c c c c c c

c

Example

o o o o o o o o

o

Example

u u u u u u u u

u

10.2 - Pond Animals

10.3 Vocabulary Worksheet

Name _____.

Vocabulary Word Crossword - *Pond Animals*

Directions: Use the definitions to complete the crossword puzzle using your vocabulary words.

Down:

1. worried or troubled
3. asked about

Across:

2. having style, fashionable
4. a variety or collection of different things
5. made happy
6. tried to persuade

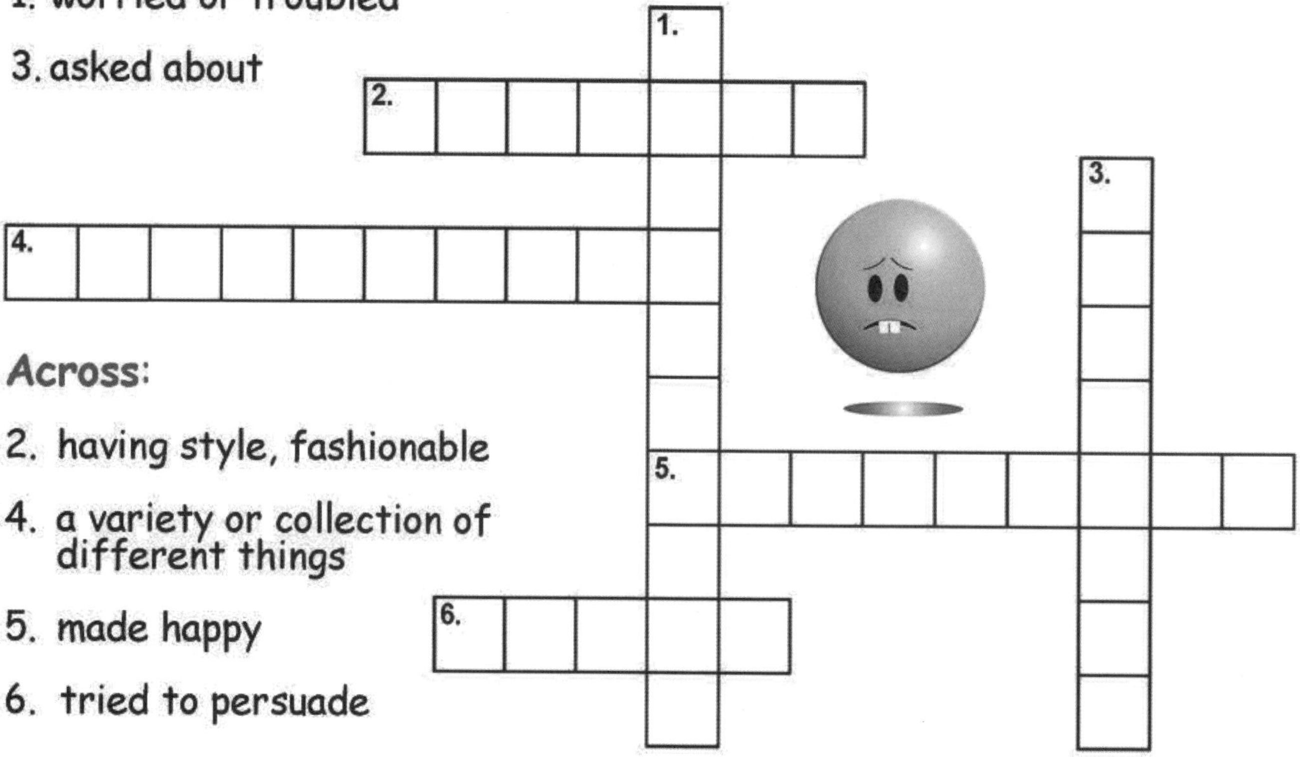

156

10.3 - Pond Animals

10.4 Spelling Worksheet

Name _____.

Fill in the Blanks - *Pond Animals*

Directions: Fill in the blanks to spell each word.

1) thr ☐ ☐

2) thr ☐ ☐ ☐

3) thr ☐ ☐ ☐

4) thr ☐ ☐ ☐

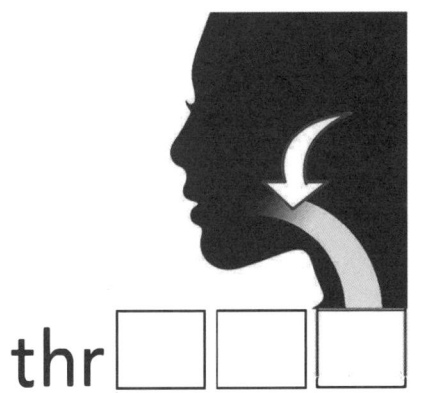

5) thr ☐ ☐

6) thr ☐ ☐ ☐

Continue on following page.

10.4 - Pond Animals

Directions: Circle the correct spelling of the word and then write the correct spelling on the blank.

1. here   hre   haer   _____
2. himm   him   heem   _____
3. his   hise   hiis   _____
4. howe   hou   how   _____
5. just   juste   jost   _____
6. knou   nou   know   _____
7. lett   let   leet   _____
8. liv   liev   live   _____
9. maye   maey   may   _____
10. ov   of   ove   _____
11. old   olde   ould   _____
12. once   ounc   onse   _____

10.4 - Pond Animals

10.4 Grammar Worksheet

Name _____ .

Verbs - Pond Animals

Directions:
Fill in the blank using the correct **future tense** form of the verb in parenthesis.

1. I _____ (run) as fast as I can in tomorrow's race.

2. She _____ (sing) her solo at the concert this weekend.

3. Do you think we _____ (win) the game?

4. I don't think he _____ (lose) the game.

5. She said she _____ (call) me tomorrow.

6. He _____ (choose) a new book at the library.

Directions: Write a sentence using the **future tense** of the verb given.

1. swim

_____

2. stand

_____

3. bring

_____

10.4 - Pond Animals 159

10.4 Writing Checklist

Name _____.

Opinion Paragraph Checklist - *Pond Animals*

Directions: Reread your writing carefully. Put a check in each box under Author as you complete each item. Once all the boxes are checked, your teacher will check your paragraph.

Revise and Edit for the following:	Author	Teacher
1. **Clarity and Meaning** **Ask yourself,** "Does the paragraph compare and contrast two items?" "Are the similarities and differences clear?" "Are my topic sentence and conclusion clear?" Rewrite parts that need revision.		

Revise and Edit for the following:	Author	Teacher
2. **Correct Use of Words** **Ask yourself,** "Are specific similarities and differences listed?" "Are explanations used when needed?" "Do the sentences sound good together?" Rewrite parts that need revision.		

Revise and Edit for the following:	Author	Teacher
3. **Capitalization** Use capitals at the beginning of each sentence and for every name. Make corrections if needed.		

Continue on the next page.

Revise and Edit for the following:	Author	Teacher

4. Punctuation
 	
    Use periods, exclamation points, and question marks.
 	
    Use quotation marks for dialogue.
 	
    Make corrections if needed.		

Revise and Edit for the following:	Author	Teacher

5. Spelling
 	
    Check for correct spelling.
 	
    Make corrections if needed.		

Name _____.

Handwriting - Pond Animals

Directions:
Use the grey lines to help you write each letter on the first line. Continue writing each letter on your own on the following lines.

Handwriting Practice 2

a a a a a a a a

a

a

c

c

o

o

u

u

Name _____.

Spelling - *Pond Animals*

Spelling Test

Directions:
As your teacher reads your words, write each spelling word on the blanks below.

1) _____

2) _____

3) _____

4) _____

5) _____

6) _____

7) _____

8) _____

9) _____

10) _____

11) _____

12) _____

13) _____

14) _____

15) _____

16) _____

17) _____

18) _____

10.5 Reading Graphic Organizer

My name is _____

Reading - Pond Animals

Directions: Compare and contrast Paddy and Solomon from this week's stories.

Paddy | Both | Solomon

164   10.5 - Pond Animals

10.5 Independent Reading

Name _____.

Reading - *Pond Animals*

Directions: Read your independent reading book for 30 minutes. When you are done, write a short summary of what you have read.

I read _____ by _____
              (book title)   (author)

for 30 minutes today.

_____   _____
             My Signature   Parent/Guardian Signature

Write a short summary about what you read today.   **Details**

_____

_____

_____

_____

_____

_____

_____

10.5 - Pond Animals

Name _____

Journal Entry - Animal Friends

Directions: Write your response to the prompt on the lines below. Don't forget to check for complete sentences as you write.

Prompt: If you could have any animal as a pet, what would you choose? Why?

11.1 - Animal Friends

Name _____.

Spelling - *Animal Friends*

11.2 Spelling Worksheet

Rainbow Words

Directions:
Please choose three different colored pencils. Write each spelling word three times using each color.

open _____ _____ _____

over _____ _____ _____

round _____ _____ _____

some _____ _____ _____

stop _____ _____ _____

thank _____ _____ _____

them _____ _____ _____

then _____ _____ _____

think _____ _____ _____

walk _____ _____ _____

food _____ _____ _____

mood _____ _____ _____

Continue on the next page.

11.2 - Animal Friends

noodle _____ _____ _____

moon _____ _____ _____

spoon _____ _____ _____

boot _____ _____ _____

zoo _____ _____ _____

goose _____ _____ _____

poodle _____ _____ _____

raccoon _____ _____ _____

Name _____.

Writing Graphic Organizer - *Animal Friends*

Descriptive Paragraph Prewrite

Directions: Choose an animal to write a descriptive paragraph about. It can be your pet, a friend's pet or even an animal you enjoy visiting at the zoo or pet store. After you choose your animal, answer the questions below.

Animal: _____

How do you know this animal?   Details
_____
- -
_____
- -
_____

What does the animal look and feel like?   Details
_____
- -
_____
- -
_____

How does the animal act?   Details
_____
- -
_____
- -
_____

How does the animal make you feel?   Details
_____
- -
_____
- -
_____

11.2 - Animal Friends

Handwriting Practice 1

Name _____.

Handwriting - *Animal Friends*

Directions:
Use the grey lines to help you write each letter on the first line.
Continue writing each letter on your own on the following lines.

Example

Example

170

11.2 - Animal Friends

11.3 Vocabulary Worksheet

Name _____.

Vocabulary Word Crossword – *Animal Friends*

Directions: Use the definitions to complete the crossword puzzle using your vocabulary words.

Across:
2. tired of waiting for something
5. ate up greedily or hungrily
6. gloomily or resentfully silent

Down:
1. failed to see or missed
3. having a liking or love
4. bent, twisted, or turned unusually to one side

11.3 - Animal Friends

Name _____.

11.4 Spelling Worksheet

Fill in the Blanks - *Animal Friends*

Directions: Fill in the blanks to spell each word.

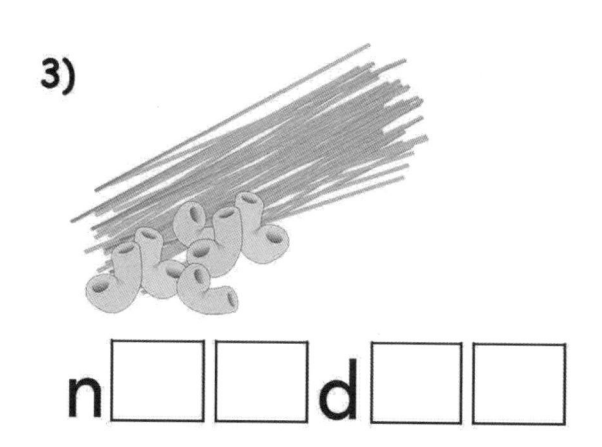

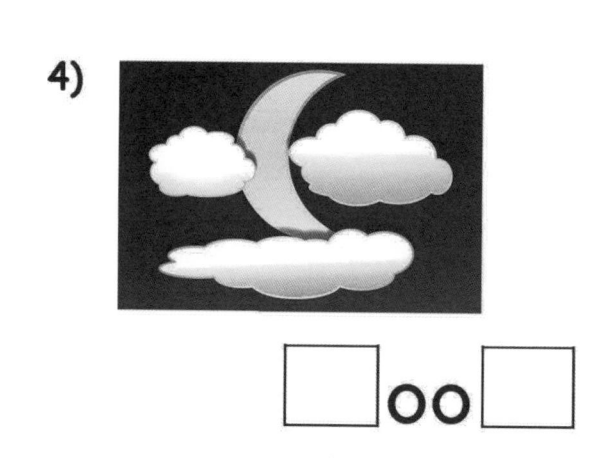

1) fo☐☐

2) ☐☐od

3) n☐☐d☐☐

4) ☐oo☐

5) s☐oo☐

6) bo☐☐

Continue on following page.

172

11.4 - Animal Friends

7) ☐☐o

8) g☐☐se

9) poo☐☐☐

10) r☐☐☐oon

Directions: Circle the correct spelling of the word and then write the correct spelling on the blank.

Circle Correct Spelling			Write Correct Word
1. opin	open	opun	_____
2. ovur	ovar	over	_____
3. round	ruond	rund	_____
4. some	som	sume	_____
5. stopp	stop	stoup	_____
6. thank	thaenk	thenk	_____

Continue on following page.

11.4 - Animal Friends

7. themm   tem   them   _____

8. then   thenn   thean   _____

9. thenk   think   tinke   _____

10. walk   walke   wak   _____

11.4 Grammar Worksheet

Name _____.

Pronouns - *Animal Friends*

Directions:
Rewrite each sentence. Change the word or words in parentheses to a **pronoun**.

1. (**Sarah**) forgot her homework today.

_____

_____

2. Tyler played cards with (**Mike and Jordan**).

_____

_____

3. Mr. Jennings went to the party with (**Mrs. Jennings**).

_____

_____

4. (**The room**) needs a fresh coat of paint.

_____

_____

5. Sasha will get a ride from (**Michele's parents**).

_____

_____

6. (**Olivia**) has a beautiful singing voice.

_____

_____

11.4 - Animal Friends

11.4 Writing Checklist

Name _____

Descriptive Paragraph Checklist
- Animal Friends

Directions: Reread your writing carefully. Put a check in each box under **Author** as you complete each item. Once all the boxes are checked, submit your work to your teacher for the final check.

Revise and Edit for the following:	Author	Teacher
1. Clarity and Meaning *Ask yourself,* "Does the paragraph describe the animal?" "Are the details clear and did I include enough of them?" Rewrite parts that need revision.		

Revise and Edit for the following:	Author	Teacher
2. Correct Use of Words *Ask yourself,* "Are specific details and words used?" "Are explanations used when needed?" "Do the sentences sound good together?" Rewrite parts that need revision.		

Revise and Edit for the following:	Author	Teacher
3. Capitalization Use capitals at the beginning of each sentence and for every name. Make corrections if needed.		

Continue on the next page.

Revise and Edit for the following:	Author	Teacher

4. Punctuation
     Use periods, exclamation points, and question marks.
     Use quotation marks for dialogue.
     Make corrections if needed.		

Revise and Edit for the following:	Author	Teacher

5. Spelling
     Check for correct spelling.
     Make corrections if needed.		

Handwriting Practice 2

Name _____.

Handwriting - *Animal Friends*

Directions:
Use the grey lines to help you write each letter on the first line.
Continue writing each letter on your own on the following lines.

Example

178   11.4 - Animal Friends

Name _____.

Spelling - *Animal Friends*

Directions:
As your teacher reads your words, write each spelling word on the blanks below.

Spelling Test

1) _____
2) _____
3) _____
4) _____
5) _____
6) _____
7) _____
8) _____
9) _____
10) _____

11) _____
12) _____
13) _____
14) _____
15) _____
16) _____
17) _____
18) _____
19) _____
20) _____

11.5 - Animal Friends

11.5 Independent Reading

Name _____.

Reading - *Animal Friends*

Directions: Read your independent reading book for 30 minutes. When you are done, write a short summary of what you have read.

I read _____ by _____
     (book title)   (author)

for 30 minutes today.

_____   _____
    My Signature   Parent/Guardian Signature

Write a short summary about what you read today.   **Details**

_____

_____

_____

_____

_____

_____

_____

180   11.5 - Animal Friends

Name _____

Journal Entry - *Night Animals*

Directions: Write your response to the prompt on the lines below. Don't forget to check for complete sentences as you write.

Prompt: Night animals are nocturnal. They stay up at night and sleep during the day. Imagine that you were nocturnal. What would you do at night?

12.1 - Night Animals   181

Name _____.

Spelling - *Night Animals*

Rainbow Words

Directions:
Please choose three different colored pencils. Write each spelling word three times using each color.

were _____ _____ _____

when _____ _____ _____

always _____ _____ _____

around _____ _____ _____

because _____ _____ _____

been _____ _____ _____

before _____ _____ _____

best _____ _____ _____

both _____ _____ _____

buy _____ _____ _____

call _____ _____ _____

cold _____ _____ _____

Continue on the next page.

crawl _____ _____ _____

lawn _____ _____ _____

yawn _____ _____ _____

hawk _____ _____ _____

author _____ _____ _____

haunt _____ _____ _____

pause _____ _____ _____

sauce _____ _____ _____

12.2 - Night Animals

My name is _____.

12.2 Writing Graphic Organizer
Paragraph Prewrite – Night Animals

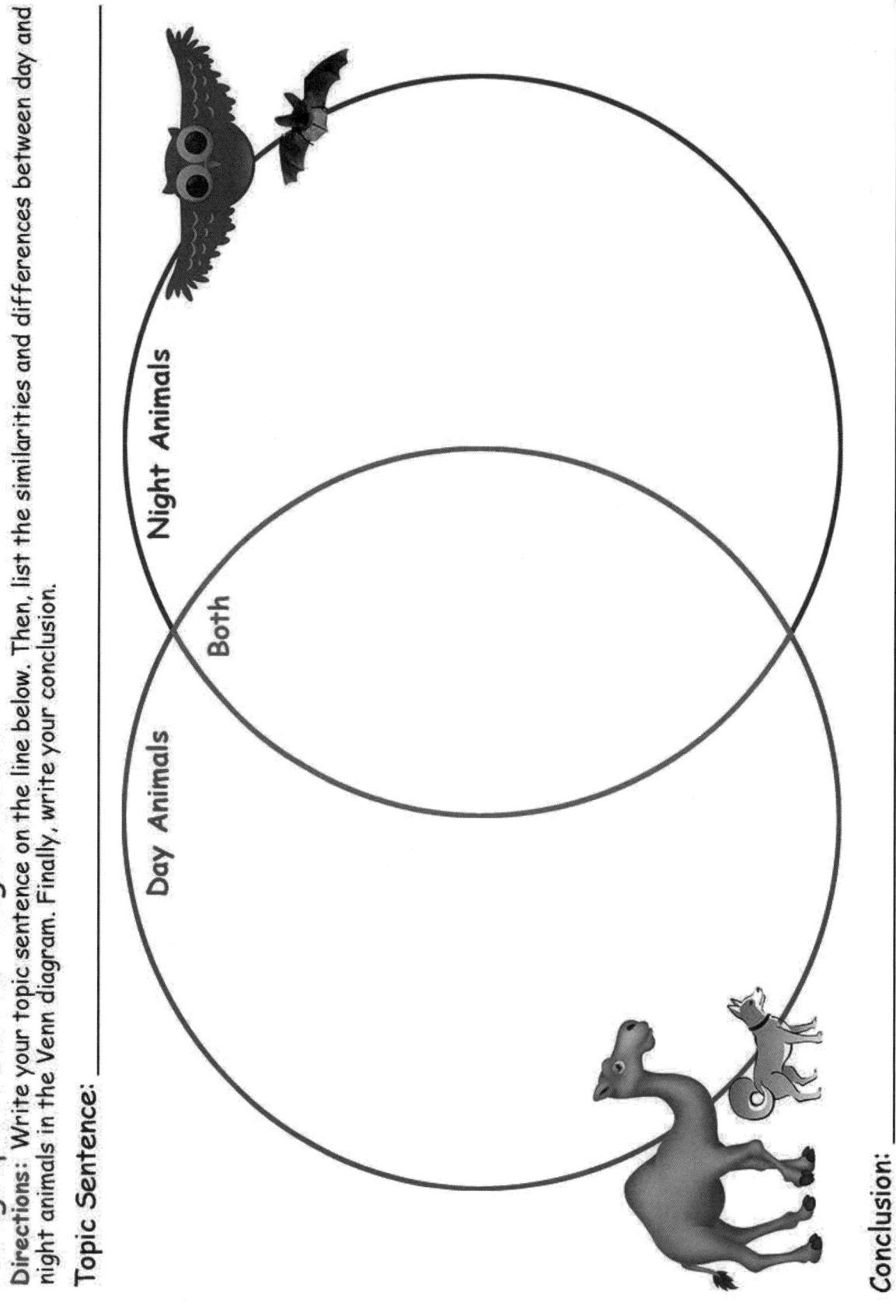

Directions: Write your topic sentence on the line below. Then, list the similarities and differences between day and night animals in the Venn diagram. Finally, write your conclusion.

Topic Sentence: _____

Night Animals

Both

Day Animals

Conclusion: _____

184   12.2 - Night Animals

Handwriting Practice 1

Name _____

Handwriting - *Night Animals*

Directions:
Use the grey lines to help you write each letter on the first line. Continue writing each letter on your own on the following lines.

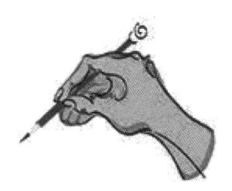

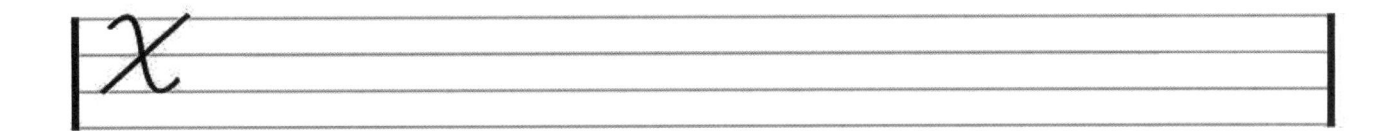

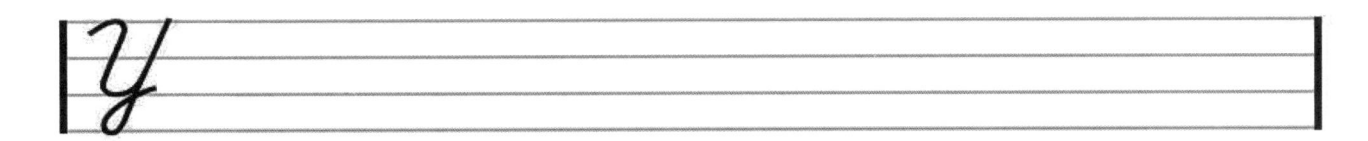

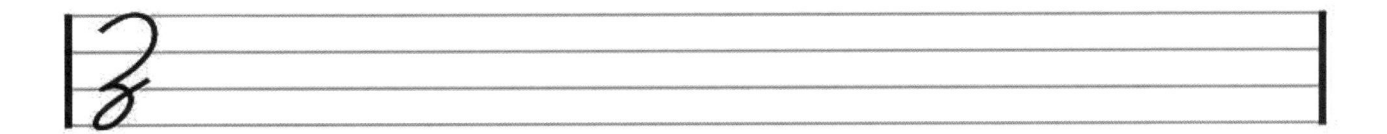

Example

Example

Example

12.2 - Night Animals

185

12.3 Vocabulary Worksheet

Name _____.

Vocabulary Word Crossword - Night Animals

Directions: Use the definitions to complete the crossword puzzle using your vocabulary words.

Across:
2. very dreary and depressing
3. a sheltered or hidden place
5. a small piece of food

Down:
1. partial or total darkness
2. an argument or debate
4. to go from place to place without a plan

12.4 Spelling Worksheet

Name _____

Fill in the Blanks - *Night Animals*

Directions: Fill in the blanks to spell each word.

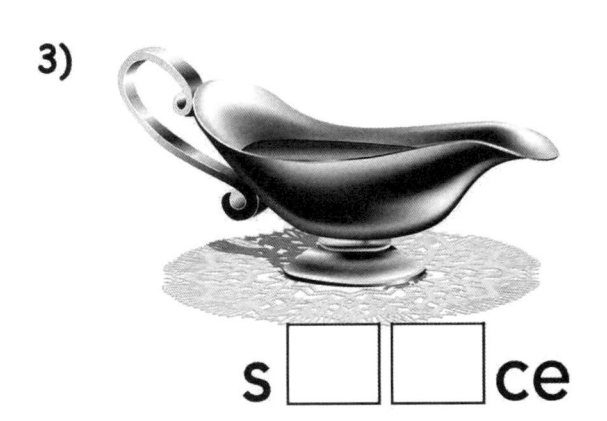

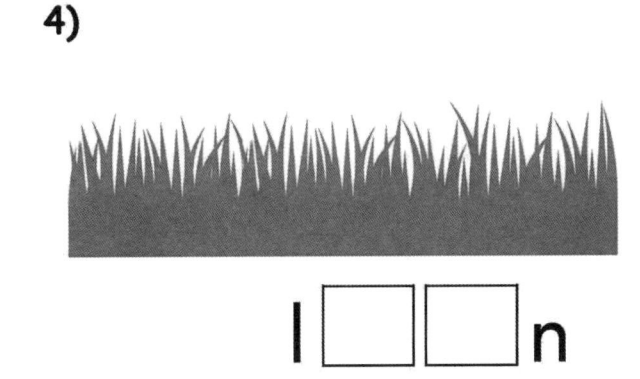

1) cr☐☐l

2) h☐☐nt

3) s☐☐ce

4) l☐☐n

5) y☐☐n

6) ☐☐thor

Continue on following page.

12.4 - Night Animals

7) p☐☐se

8) h☐☐k

Directions: Circle the correct spelling of the word and then write the correct spelling on the blank.

Circle Correct Spelling			Write Correct Word
1. were	wur	wer	_____
2. wen	ween	when	_____
3. always	aways	allways	_____
4. aronde	around	eround	_____
5. becase	becaus	because	_____
6. ben	bene	been	_____
7. before	befor	befour	_____
8. beste	beest	best	_____
9. bothe	bouth	both	_____
10. buye	buy	buuy	_____
11. cal	call	cale	_____
12. cold	coulde	colde	_____

12.4 - Night Animals

Name _____.

Reading - *Night Animals*

12.4 Reading Worksheet

Benjamin Bat

Directions: Please answer the question below after reading "**Benjamin Bat**." Circle the correct answer.

1. Why does Benjamin Bat need somewhere to stay?
    a. His home was destroyed.
    b. There is a storm coming.
    c. He doesn't have a home.

2. Why is Benjamin Bat nervous about staying with Solomon Owl?
    a. Solomon tried to catch him and eat him before.
    b. Solomon was very mean and didn't want Benjamin to stay with him.
    c. Benjamin is afraid he won't get any sleep there.

3. Why can't Solomon find Benjamin in the middle of the afternoon?
    a. Benjamin flew home.
    b. Benjamin was hanging from the ceiling.
    c. Benjamin was hiding under a pile of leaves.

4. What did Benjamin learn about Solomon Owl?
_____
_____
_____

12.4 - Night Animals 189

12.4 Grammar Worksheet

Name _____

Pronouns - Night Animals

Directions:
For each of the following sentences, circle the correct **pronoun** from the parenthesis. Also underline the **antecedent**.

1. Hayley and (**her, their**) friends wanted to go roller skating.

2. Before Hayley left, (**she, they**) finished her chores.

3. Hayley's older brother said (**he, they**) would take Hayley.

4. When Hayley and her brother go into the car, (**their, they**) talked about skating.

5. Hayley's brother and (**his, their**) best friend skate often.

6. Hayley hopes that (**she, their**) won't fall.

7. Hayley put on her skates and glided (**herself, she**) onto the rink.

12.4 Writing Checklist

Name _____

Compare and Contrast Paragraph Checklist

Directions: Reread your writing carefully. Put a check in each box under **Author** as you complete each item. Once all the boxes are checked, your **peer partner** will check your paragraph and put a check in each box.

Revise and Edit for the following:	Author	Peer Partner
1. Clarity and Meaning **Ask yourself,** "Does the paragraph compare and contrast day and night animals?" "Are the similarities and differences clear?" "Are the topic sentence and conclusion clear?" Rewrite parts that need revision.		

Revise and Edit for the following:	Author	Peer Partner
2. Correct Use of Words **Ask yourself,** "Are specific similarities and differences listed?" "Are explanations used when needed?" "Do the sentences sound good together?"" Rewrite parts that need revision.		

Revise and Edit for the following:	Author	Peer Partner
3. Capitalization Use capitals at the beginning of each sentence and for every name. Make corrections if needed.		

Continue on the next page.

12.4 - Night Animals

Revise and Edit for the following:	Author	Peer Partner
4. Punctuation 　　Use periods, exclamation points, and question marks. 　　Make corrections if needed.		

Revise and Edit for the following:	Author	Peer Partner
5. Spelling 　　Check for correct spelling. 　　Make corrections if needed.		

Handwriting Practice 2

Name _____.

Handwriting - *Night Animals*

Directions:
Use the grey lines to help you write each letter on the first line. Continue writing each letter on your own on the following lines.

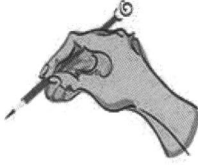

Example

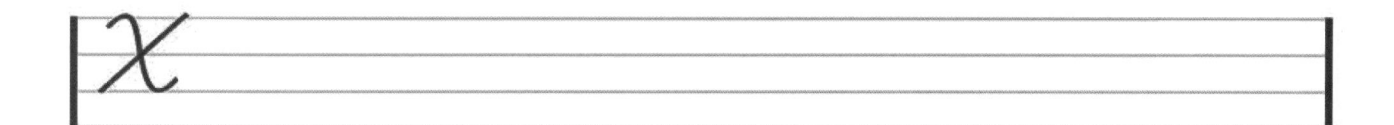

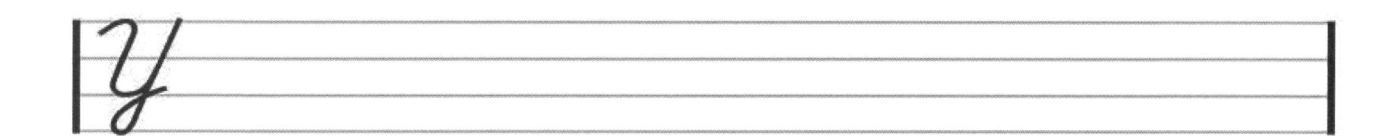

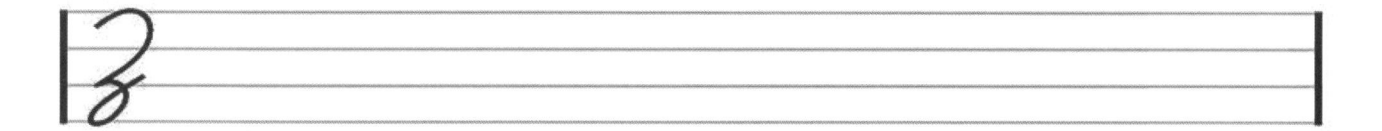

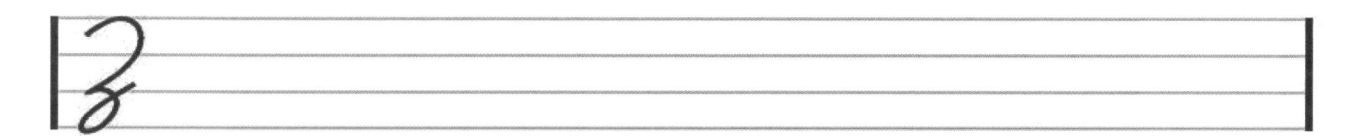

x x x x x x x x

x

x

y

y

z

z

12.4 - Night Animals

Name _____

Spelling - *Night Animals*

Spelling Test

Directions:
As your teacher reads your words, write each spelling word on the blanks below.

1) _____   11) _____

2) _____   12) _____

3) _____   13) _____

4) _____   14) _____

5) _____   15) _____

6) _____   16) _____

7) _____   17) _____

8) _____   18) _____

9) _____   19) _____

10) _____   20) _____

12.5 - Night Animals

12.5 Independent Reading

Name _____.

Reading - *Night Animals*

Directions: Read your independent reading book for 30 minutes. When you are done, compare and contrast this book with another one that you have read.

I read _____ by _____
      (book title)   (author)

for 30 minutes today.

_____   _____
My Signature   Parent/Guardian Signature

Compare and contrast this book with another one that you have read.

Details

_____
_____
_____
_____
_____
_____
_____
_____

12.5 - Night Animals

Name _____.

Journal Entry - *Rural vs. City*

Directions: Write your response to the prompt on the lines below. Don't forget to check for complete sentences as you write.

Prompt: Describe where you live. Is it a city, the country, or somewhere in between? Use details to describe it.

_____
_____
_____
_____
_____
_____
_____
_____
_____
_____
_____
_____
_____
_____
_____

13.1 - Rural vs. City

Name _____

Spelling - *Rural vs. City*

13.2 Spelling Worksheet

Rainbow Words

Directions:
Please choose three different colored pencils. Write each spelling word three times using each color.

does   _____   _____   _____

fast   _____   _____   _____

first   _____   _____   _____

five   _____   _____   _____

found   _____   _____   _____

gave   _____   _____   _____

goes   _____   _____   _____

green   _____   _____   _____

its   _____   _____   _____

made   _____   _____   _____

many   _____   _____   _____

off   _____   _____   _____

Continue on the next page.

13.2 - Rural vs. City

knife _____ _____ _____

knew _____ _____ _____

knight _____ _____ _____

thumb _____ _____ _____

doubt _____ _____ _____

tomb _____ _____ _____

My name is _____.

13.2 Writing Graphic Organizer

Compare and Contrast Paragraph Prewrite - *Rural vs. City*

Directions: Write your topic sentence on the line below. Then, list the similarities and differences between rural and city life in the Venn diagram. Finally, write your conclusion.

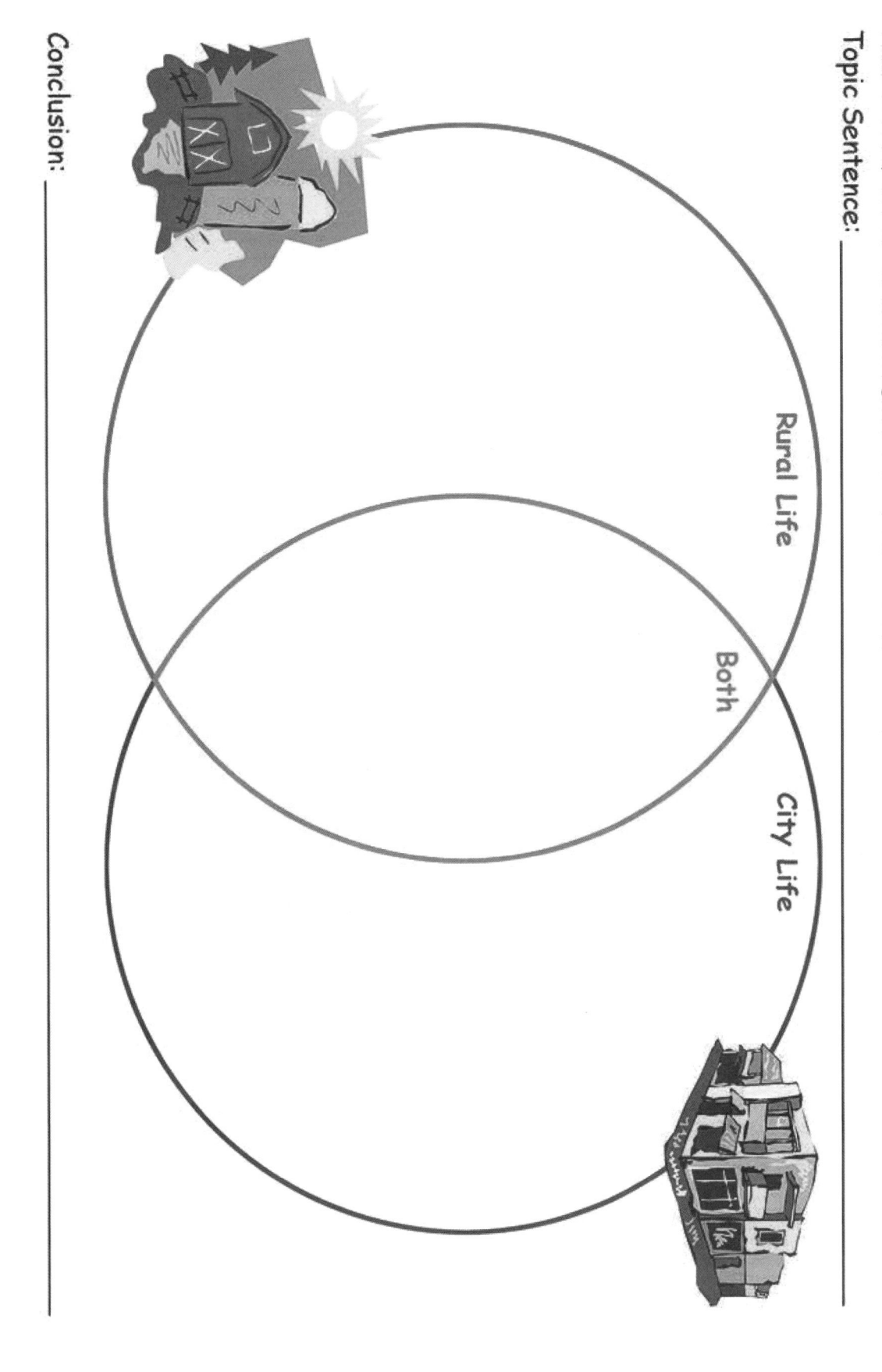

Topic Sentence: _____

Rural Life

Both

City Life

Conclusion: _____

13.2 - Rural vs. City

199

Name _____

Handwriting - Rural vs. City

Handwriting Practice 1

Directions: Use the grey lines to help write each letter on the first line and continue writing each letter on your own on the second line.

Example

P P P P P P P P

P

Example

B B B B B B B B

B

Example

R R R R R R R R

R

13.2 - Rural vs. City

Name _____

13.3 Vocabulary Worksheet

Vocabulary - *Rural vs. Urban*

Directions: Match each word with the correct definition.

1. city   to have in mind as a purpose or aim

2. dull   slow in action, uninteresting

3. intend   the state of being in self control and calm

4. patience   to keep from happening

5. rural   a place in which people live that is larger or more important than a town

6. avoid   of or relating to the country

Directions: Use context clues to determine the meaning of these new words.

1. A lutat is a simple drawing of part or all of the earth. Most lutats are flat. Lutats show only the important details such as names of places. The lutat key explains what the lutat symbols mean. For example, a black dot may stand for a city.

What does the word lutat mean in this paragraph? _____

_____

_____

1. What is today's murp like? Is it hot, rainy, or sunny? It can be fun to make a murp chart. Record the high and low temperatures for each day of the week. Listen or watch a murp report on television or radio to get the prediction for tomorrow's murp!

What does the word murp mean in this paragraph? _____

_____

_____

13.3 - Rural vs. City   201

13.4 Spelling Worksheet

Name _____.

Silent Letters K and B -
Rural vs. City

Directions: Sort the spelling words in the word bank into the correct category below.

WORD BANK:

| knife | thumb | tomb |
| knew | doubt | knight |

Silent **k**	Silent **b**

Directions: Write each spelling word two times.

1) does _____ _____

2) fast _____ _____

3) first _____ _____

4) five _____ _____

5) found _____ _____

6) gave _____ _____

7) goes _____ _____

Continue on the next page.

202   13.4 - Rural vs. City

8) green _____ _____

9) its _____ _____

10) made _____ _____

11) many _____ _____

12) off _____ _____

13.4 - Rural vs. City

Name _____

13.4 Reading Worksheet

Reading - Rural vs. City

Aiden's Big Move
—
City Gardens

Directions: Please answer the questions below after reading "**Aiden's Big Move**" and "**City Gardens**." Circle the correct answer.

1. What was Aiden's reaction when he first learned that he would be moving?
    a. He was upset.
    b. He was excited.
    c. He didn't care.

2. What does Aiden notice when he pulls into his new driveway?
    a. There are no other houses anywhere.
    b. There are kids playing a few houses away.
    c. His new house is a farm with cows, pigs, and horses.

3. How do you think you would have felt about this move if you were Aiden?

_____

_____

_____

4. What are some tips for starting a garden in the city?

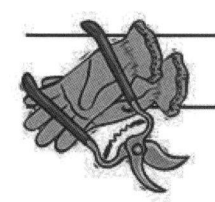

_____

_____

_____

13.4 - Rural vs. City

13.4 Grammar Worksheet

Name _____.

Grammar - *Rural vs. City*

Directions: For each of the following sentences, insert commas to separate the items in a series.

The butcher, the baker,
The candlestick maker,

,,, Series Commas:

1. I enjoy reading collecting shells and riding waves at the beach.

2. I put sprinkles chocolate chips and strawberries on my ice cream.

3. Her family has a rabbit two cats and a dog.

4. I rode my bike to the playground with Kevin Colin and Sheila.

5. I got a new book some clothes and a new game for my birthday.

Articles:

Directions: Circle the correct article to complete each sentence below.

1. (A, An) deer walked across our front lawn this morning.

2. I have (a, an) apple in my lunch today.

3. (A, An) airplane flew through (the, a) clouds.

4. I saw (a, an) little girl playing with (a, an) ball.

5. (A, An) boy was flying (a, an) kite.

13.4 - Rural vs. City   205

13.4 Writing Checklist

Name _____.

Compare and Contrast Paragraph Checklist

Directions: Reread your writing carefully. Put a check in each box under **Author** as you complete each item. Once all the boxes are checked, submit your work to your **teacher** for the final check.

Revise and Edit for the following:	Author	Teacher
1. Clarity and Meaning **Ask yourself,** "Does the paragraph compare and contrast rural and city life?" "Are the similarities and differences clear?" "Are my topic sentence and conclusion clear?" Rewrite parts that need revision.		

Revise and Edit for the following:	Author	Teacher
2. Correct Use of Words **Ask yourself,** "Are specific similarities and differences listed?" "Are explanations used when needed?" "Do the sentences sound good together?" Rewrite parts that need revision.		

Revise and Edit for the following:	Author	Teacher
3. Capitalization Use capitals at the beginning of each sentence and for every name. Make corrections if needed.		

Continue on the next page.

Revise and Edit for the following:	Author	Teacher

4. Punctuation
 	
   Use periods, exclamation points, and question marks.
 	
   Make corrections if needed.		

Revise and Edit for the following:	Author	Teacher

5. Spelling
 	
   Check for correct spelling.
 	
   Make corrections if needed.		

Handwriting Practice 2

Name _____.

Handwriting - Rural vs. City

Directions: Use the grey lines to help write each letter on the first line and continue writing each letter on your own on the second line.

Example

P P P P P P P P P

P

P

B

B

R

R

Name _____.

Spelling - *Rural vs. City*

Directions:
As your teacher reads your words, write each spelling word on the blanks below.

Spelling Test

1) _____
2) _____
3) _____
4) _____
5) _____
6) _____
7) _____
8) _____
9) _____
10) _____

11) _____
12) _____
13) _____
14) _____
15) _____
16) _____
17) _____
18) _____

13.5 Independent Reading

Name _____

Reading - *Rural vs. City*

Directions: Read your independent reading book for 30 minutes. When you are done, write a short summary of what you read today.

I read _____ by _____
             (book title)   (author)

for 30 minutes today.

_____   _____
My Signature   Parent/Guardian Signature

Write a short summary of what you read today.

_____ Details

_____

_____

_____

_____

_____

_____

_____

13.5 - Rural vs. City

Name _____.

Journal Entry - *Jobs in the Community*

Directions: Write your response to the prompt on the lines below. Don't forget to check for complete sentences as you write.

Prompt: If you had to take on a job in your community, what would it be? Why?

14.1 - Jobs in the Community

Name _____.

Spelling - *Jobs in the Community*

14.2 Spelling Worksheet

Rainbow Words

Directions:
Please choose three different colored pencils. Write each spelling word three times using each color.

or	_____	_____	_____
pull	_____	_____	_____
read	_____	_____	_____
right	_____	_____	_____
sing	_____	_____	_____
sit	_____	_____	_____
sleep	_____	_____	_____
tell	_____	_____	_____
their	_____	_____	_____
these	_____	_____	_____
those	_____	_____	_____
upon	_____	_____	_____

Continue on the next page.

toil   _____   _____   _____

noisy   _____   _____   _____

point   _____   _____   _____

oyster _____   _____   _____

royal   _____   _____   _____

destroy _____   _____   _____

14.2 - Jobs in the Community

Name _____

Paragraph Writing -
Jobs in the Community

Cause and Effect Prewrite

Directions: Complete the graphic organizer below using information you know about jobs in the community.

In the "Cause" box, write what the community needs (Example – Communities need someone to enforce rules).

In the "Effect" box, write what job is created because of that need (Example – Police officers are hired).

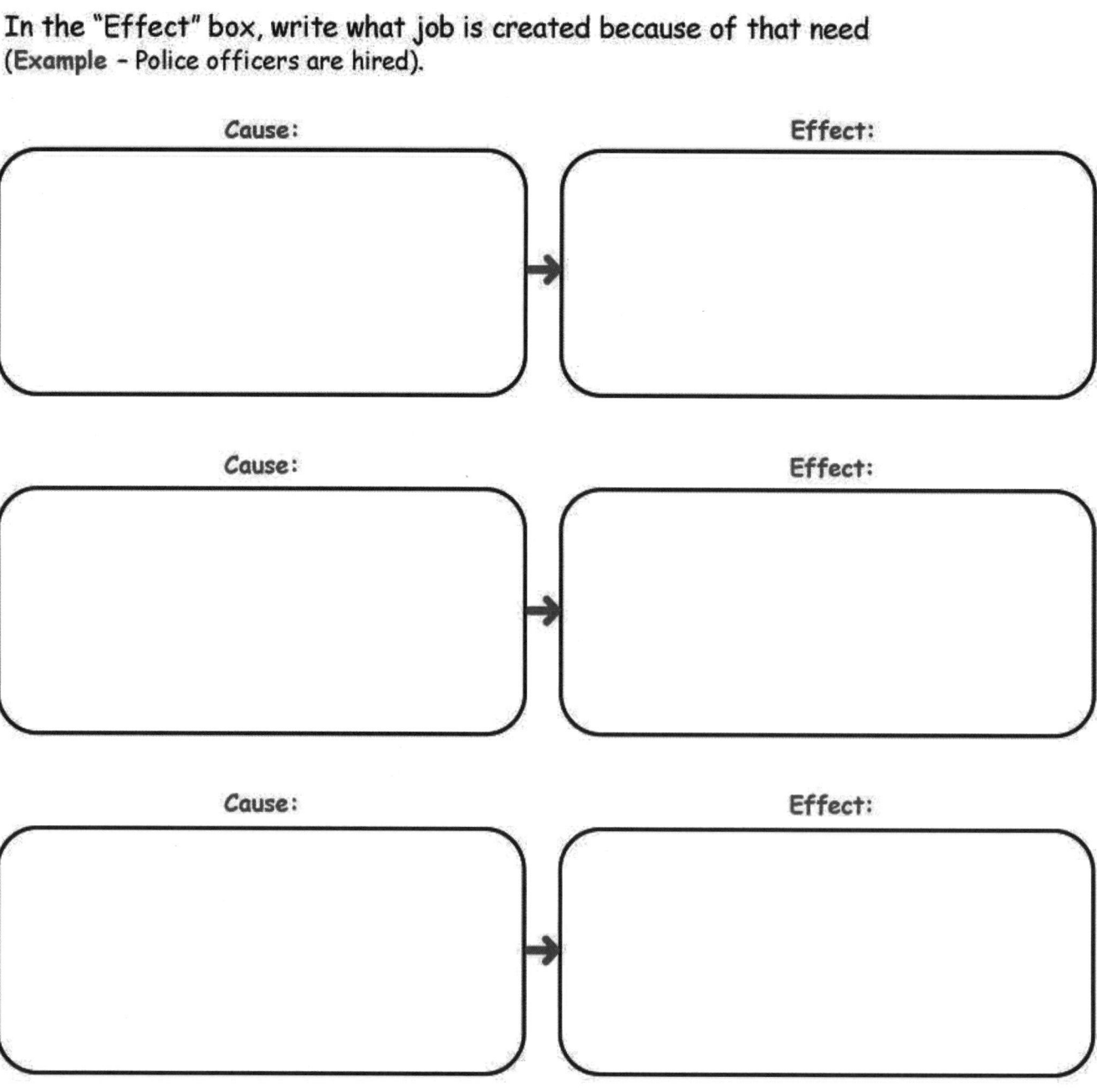

Cause: → **Effect:**

Cause: → **Effect:**

Cause: → **Effect:**

Name _____.

Handwriting - *Jobs in the Community*

Directions:
Use the grey lines to help you write each letter on the first line. Continue writing each letter on your own on the following lines.

Example

n n n n n n n n

n

Example

m m m m m m m m

m

Example

s s s s s s s s

s s s s s s s s

s

14.2 - Jobs in the Community

Name _____

14.3 Vocabulary Worksheet

Vocabulary - *Jobs in the Community*

Directions: Match each word with the correct definition.

1. responsible   the quality or state of being able

2. average   carry out, do

3. resident   being the one who must answer or account for something

4. ability   one who lives in a place

5. perform   the value found by adding all numbers in a set together and dividing them by the amount of numbers in the set

6. prevent   to keep from happening

Directions: Match the **idiom** on the left with its meaning on the right.

To have butterflies in your stomach   To be sad

To hit the hay   Go ahead and eat

You're driving me up a wall   You're bothering me

Chow down   Good luck

Break a leg   To be nervous

Down in the dumps   To go to bed

216   14.3 - Jobs in the Community

14.4 Spelling Worksheet

Name _____

Fill in the Blanks - *Jobs in the Community*

Directions: Fill in the blanks to spell each word.

1) t ☐ ☐ l

2) n ☐ ☐ sy

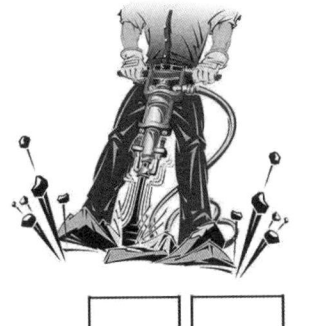

3) r ☐ ☐ al

4) ☐ ☐ ster

5) destr ☐ ☐

6) p ☐ ☐ nt

Continue on following page.

14.4 - Jobs in the Community 217

Directions: Write each spelling word two times.

1) or _____ _____

2) pull _____ _____

3) read _____ _____

4) right _____ _____

5) sing _____ _____

6) sit _____ _____

7) sleep _____ _____

8) tell _____ _____

9) their _____ _____

10) these _____ _____

11) those _____ _____

12) upon _____ _____

Name _____

Reading - Jobs in the Community

14.4 Reading Worksheet

Jobs in the Community

Directions: Please answer these questions after reading "**Jobs in the Community**". Circle the correct answer.

1. Who helps the mayor create local laws?
    a. the president
    b. the city council
    c. police officers

2. If someone in your community is building a new home, who would you find on site?
    a. a contractor
    b. a fire fighter
    c. the mayor

3. Who isn't paid for the work that they do?
    a. a volunteer
    b. a teacher
    c. a fire fighter

4. If you had to perform one of the jobs we read about in "**Jobs in the Community**," which would you choose? Why?

_____
_____
_____
_____

14.4 - Jobs in the Community   219

14.4 Grammar Worksheet

Name _____.

Grammar – *Jobs in the Community*

Directions: For each sentence below, underline the **subject** once and the **predicate** twice.

1. Jill is reading a fantasy book.

2. Noah rides his bike to school each day.

3. Sarah and I are leaving for camp tomorrow.

4. My friend's dog loves to chase sticks.

5. My mom made me an ice cream sundae for dessert.

6. My brother and I made my mom a birthday cake.

7. Sarah and Kaely rode the roller coaster.

14.4 Writing Checklist

Name _____.

Opinion Paragraph Checklist - *Jobs in the Community*

Directions: Reread your writing carefully. Put a check in each box under Author as you complete each item. Once all the boxes are checked, submit your work to your teacher for the final check.

Revise and Edit for the following:	Author	Teacher
1. **Clarity and Meaning** *Ask yourself,* "Does the paragraph explain three cause and effect relationships for jobs in a community?" "Are the causes and effects clear?" "Are my topic sentence and conclusion clear?" Rewrite parts that need revision.		

Revise and Edit for the following:	Author	Teacher
2. **Correct Use of Words** *Ask yourself,* "Are specific cause and effect words used?" "Are explanations used when needed?" "Do the sentences sound good together?" Rewrite parts that need revision.		

Revise and Edit for the following:	Author	Teacher
3. **Capitalization** Use capitals at the beginning of each sentence and for every name. Make corrections if needed.		

Continue on the next page.

14.4 - Jobs in the Community

Revise and Edit for the following:	Author	Teacher

4. Punctuation
 	
    Use periods, exclamation points, and question marks.
 	
    Make corrections if needed.		

Revise and Edit for the following:	Author	Teacher

5. Spelling
 	
    Check for correct spelling.
 	
    Make corrections if needed.		

Handwriting Practice 2

Name _____.

Handwriting - *Jobs in the Community*

Directions:
Use the grey lines to help you write each letter on the first line.
Continue writing each letter on your own on the following lines.

Example

n n n n n n n n

n

n

m

m

s

s

s

14.4 - Jobs in the Community

Name _____

Spelling Test

Spelling - *Jobs in the Community*

Directions:
As your teacher reads your words, write each spelling word on the blanks below.

1) _____   11) _____

2) _____   12) _____

3) _____   13) _____

4) _____   14) _____

5) _____   15) _____

6) _____   16) _____

7) _____   17) _____

8) _____   18) _____

9) _____

10) _____

14.5 Independent Reading

Name _____.

Reading - *Jobs in Communities*

Directions: Read your independent reading book for 30 minutes. When you are done, describe a cause and effect relationship you read about.

I read _____ by _____
         (book title)   (author)

for 30 minutes today.

_____   _____
      My Signature   Parent/Guardian Signature

Describe a cause and effect relationship you read about today.

_____

_____

_____

_____

_____

_____

_____

_____

Name _____

Journal Entry - Community Leaders

Directions: Write your response to the prompt on the lines below. Don't forget to check for complete sentences as you write.

Prompt: Explain how you could make a difference in your community. What would you do? Why?

15.1 - Community Leaders

Name _____.

Spelling - *Community Leaders*

15.2 Spelling Worksheet

Rainbow Words

Directions:
Please choose three different colored pencils. Write each spelling word three times using each color.

together _____ _____ _____

us _____ _____ _____

use _____ _____ _____

very _____ _____ _____

wash _____ _____ _____

which _____ _____ _____

why _____ _____ _____

wish _____ _____ _____

work _____ _____ _____

would _____ _____ _____

write _____ _____ _____

your _____ _____ _____

Continue on the next page.

15.2 - Community Leaders

faster _____ _____ _____

bigger _____ _____ _____

louder _____ _____ _____

shorter _____ _____ _____

wisest _____ _____ _____

kindest _____ _____ _____

hottest _____ _____ _____

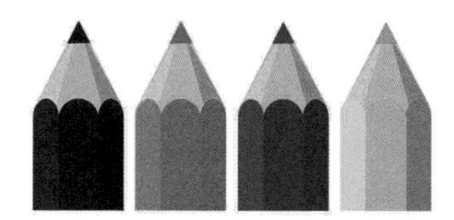

strangest _____ _____ _____

15.2 - Community Leaders

Name _____.

Writing - *Community Leaders*

Directions: Fill in the graphic organizer below with information about the person you have chosen to write a biography about.

Biography Graphic Organizer

Birth Date:
_____

Hometown:
_____

Early Life:
_____
_____
_____
_____
_____
_____

Name:
_____

Life Now:
_____
_____
_____
_____

Character Traits: (Adjectives)
_____
_____
_____
_____
_____

15.2 - Community Leaders

Name _____.

Handwriting - Community Leaders

Directions:
Use the grey lines to help you write each letter on the first line. Continue writing each letter on your own on the following lines.

Handwriting Practice 1

Example

Example

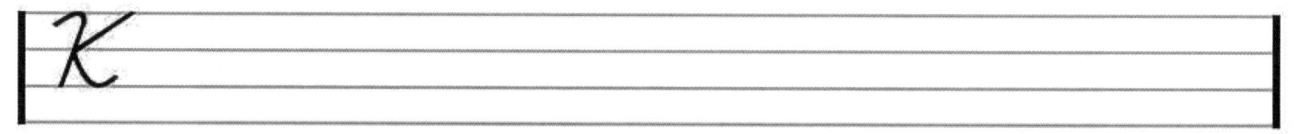

15.3 Vocabulary Worksheet

Name _____.

Vocabulary Word Crossword - Community Leaders

Directions: Use the definitions to complete the crossword puzzle using your vocabulary words.

Across:

2. something seen in the mind

5. high or special regard

6. the act of working with others to get something done

Down:

1. the object toward which effort is directed

3. an answer to a problem

4. to set apart for some purpose

15.3 - Community Leaders

15.4 Spelling Worksheet

Name _____.

Fill in the Blanks - *Community Leaders*

Directions: Fill in the blanks to spell each word.

1)  fas☐☐r

2)  bi☐☐☐r

3)  l☐☐de☐

4) shor☐☐☐

5)  wis☐☐t

6)  ki☐☐☐st

Continue on following page.

232 15.4 - Community Leaders

7) ho⬜⬜⬜st

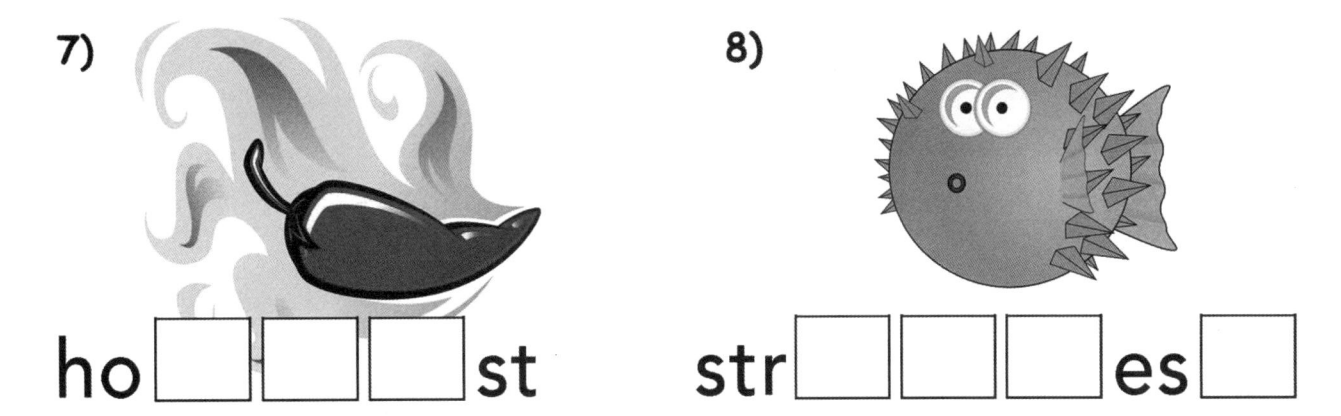

8) str⬜⬜⬜es⬜

Directions: Circle the correct spelling of the word and then write the correct spelling on the blank

Circle Correct Spelling   Write Correct Word

1) together   twogether   togethur   _____

2) uss   us   uis   _____

3) use   usse   ewse   _____

4) veri   verry   very   _____

5) washe   waesh   wash   _____

6) wich   which   wiche   _____

7) why   whi   whie   _____

8) wishe   wish   wesh   _____

9) work   wurk   werk   _____

10) would   wold   woud   _____

11) rite   write   wriet   _____

12) youre   ure   your   _____

15.4 - Community Leaders

15.4 Grammar Worksheet

Name _____.

Grammar - Community Leaders

Directions: Add the missing **quotation marks** and **punctuation** to each sentence below.

1. What is it I asked

2. We are getting a dog she exclaimed

3. Wow I shouted

4. What will we name him I asked

Directions: Fill in the blanks with the **missing adjectives**.

Adjective	Comparative	Superlative
big		
		smallest
shiny		
	fuller	
happy		
		largest

234 15.4 - Community Leaders

15.4 Writing Checklist

Name _____

Biography Checklist - Community Leaders

Directions: Reread your writing carefully. Put a check in each box under **Author** as you complete each item. Once all the boxes are checked, your **peer partner** will check your paragraph and put a check in each box.

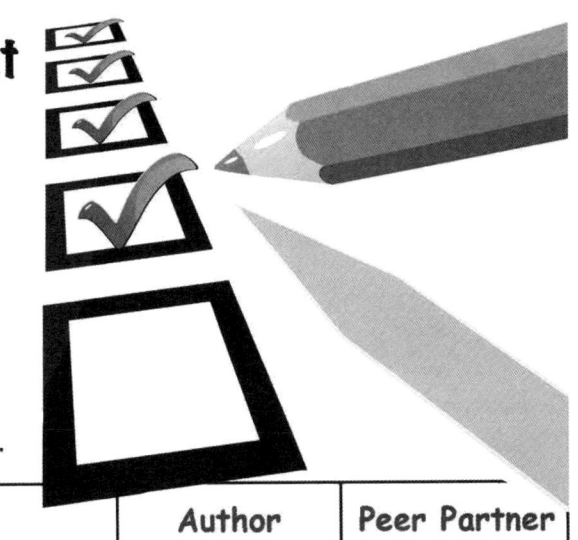

Revise and Edit for the following:	Author	Peer Partner
1. Clarity and Meaning **Ask yourself,** "Does the biography describe the person clearly?" "Are there details given about his or her life and characteristics?" "Are the topic sentence and conclusion clear?" Rewrite parts that need revision.		

Revise and Edit for the following:	Author	Peer Partner
2. Correct Use of Words **Ask yourself,** "Are specific adjectives used to describe the person?" "Are explanations used when needed?" "Do the sentences sound good together?" Rewrite parts that need revision.		

Revise and Edit for the following:	Author	Peer Partner
3. Capitalization Use capitals at the beginning of each sentence and for every name. Make corrections if needed.		

Continue on the next page.

Revise and Edit for the following:	Author	Peer Partner
4. Punctuation Use periods, exclamation points, and question marks. Make corrections if needed.		

Revise and Edit for the following:	Author	Peer Partner
5. Spelling Check for correct spelling. Make corrections if needed.		

Name _____.

Handwriting - *Community Leaders*

Handwriting Practice 2

Directions:
Use the grey lines to help you write each letter on the first line. Continue writing each letter on your own on the following lines.

Example

H H H H H H H H

H

H

H

K

K

K

15.4 - Community Leaders

Name _____

Spelling Test

Spelling - *Community Leaders*

Directions:
As your teacher reads your words, write each spelling word on the blanks below.

1) _____   11) _____

2) _____   12) _____

3) _____   13) _____

4) _____   14) _____

5) _____   15) _____

6) _____   16) _____

7) _____   17) _____

8) _____   18) _____

9) _____   19) _____

10) _____   20) _____

15.5 - Community Leaders

15.5 Reading Worksheet

Community Leaders

Name _____

Descriptive Paragraph Checklist
- Community Leaders

Directions: Write a short summary of each person below from "**Community Leaders.**"

1. Elizabeth Cady Stanton

   _____
   _____
   _____
   _____
   _____
   _____
   _____

2. Jim Thorpe

   _____
   _____
   _____
   _____
   _____
   _____

Continue on the following page.

15.5 - Community Leaders

3. Martin Luther King, Jr.

15.5 Independent Reading

Name _____.

Reading - Community Leaders

Directions: Read your independent reading book for 30 minutes. When you are done, write a short summary of what you have read.

I read _____ by _____
         (book title)   (author)

for 30 minutes today.

_____   _____
     My Signature   Parent/Guardian Signature

Write a short summary of what you read today.

_____ Details
_____
_____
_____
_____
_____
_____
_____
_____

Name _____

Journal Entry - *The Presidency*

Directions: Write your response to the prompt on the lines below. Don't forget to check for complete sentences as you write.

Prompt: If you were in charge of the United States as President, what would you change about our education system?

Name _____

Spelling - *The Presidency*

16.2 Spelling Worksheet

Rainbow Words

Directions:
Please choose three different colored pencils. Write each spelling word three times using each color.

don't   _____   _____   _____

better   _____   _____   _____

bring   _____   _____   _____

carry   _____   _____   _____

clean   _____   _____   _____

cut   _____   _____   _____

done   _____   _____   _____

draw   _____   _____   _____

drink   _____   _____   _____

eight   _____   _____   _____

fall   _____   _____   _____

far   _____   _____   _____

Continue on the next page.

16.2 - The Presidency

there _____ _____ _____

they're _____ _____ _____

their _____ _____ _____

roll _____ _____ _____

role _____ _____ _____

where _____ _____ _____

wear _____ _____ _____

ware _____ _____ _____

16.2 - The Presidency

Name _____.

Informative Paragraph Prewrite -
The Presidency

Directions: Choose one president that you are interested in learning more about. Write your president on the line below. Write a question about your president in each box below. After researching, write your answers to each question on the lines below the question boxes.

President: _____

Question 1:

Details

Answer #1: _____
_____
_____

Question 2:

Details

Answer #2: _____
_____
_____

16.2 - The Presidency

Question 3:   Details

Answer #3: _____

_____

_____

16.2 - The Presidency

Handwriting Practice 1

Name _____.

Handwriting - *The Presidency*

Directions:
Use the grey lines to help you write each letter on the first line.
Continue writing each letter on your own on the following lines.

Example

Example

Example

16.2 - The Presidency

Name _____

Vocabulary Word Crossword - The Presidency

Directions: Use the definitions to complete the crossword puzzle using your vocabulary words.

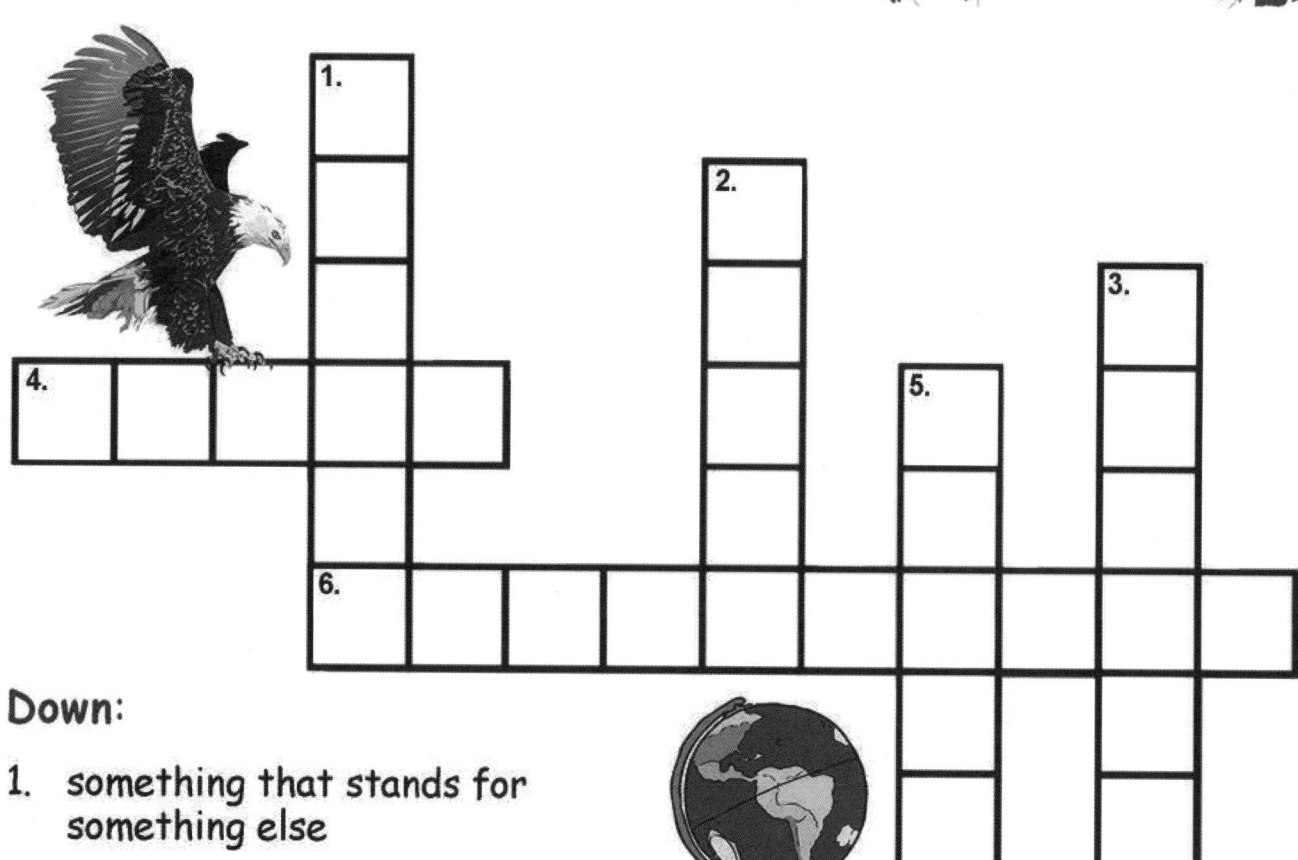

16.3 Vocabulary Worksheet

Down:

1. something that stands for something else
2. to put or come together to form a single unit
3. a large area of land controlled by its own government
5. a wise attitude, belief or course of action

Across:

4. a round object as a model of the Earth
6. a person in charge or in control

248

16.3 - The Presidency

Name _____.   **16.4 Spelling Worksheet**

Spelling - *The Presidency*

Directions: Choose a word from the box to complete each sentence. Remember that many of our spelling words are **homophones**. They sound the same but have different spellings and meanings.

don't	carry	done	eight	there	roll	wear
better	clean	draw	fall	they're	role	ware
Bring	cut	drink	far	their	Where	

1. _____ is the play performed this year?

2. They have been working on this play for _____ weeks.

3. I think it will be even_____ than the play last year.

4. Please take your seat over _____.

5. Luckily, we aren't seated _____ from the stage.

6. Do you know what _____ everyone is playing?

7. _____ me over the program and I will read it to find out.

8. I think _____ announcing each character in the program.

9. Do you know what each character will _____ from the wardrobe department?

Continue on the next page.

16.4 - The Presidency   249

10. My best friend was able to _____ pictures for the stage.

11. She _____ out different pictures to trace before coloring them.

12. I helped her _____ the pictures and other props because there were so many.

13. We arranged the props so they wouldn't _____ during the show.

14. I hope they have a _____ or some other snack to eat during intermission.

15. Then, I will need a _____ of water before the show begins again.

16. When it was _____ turn, each actor took a bow.

17. That table on stage has fancy _____ set up for the first dinner scene.

18. Please _____ talk during the show.

19. I am volunteering to _____ up the room after the show.

20. When the play is all _____, I will go back and visit with the actors.

16.4 - The Presidency

Name _____

Reading - *The Presidency*

16.4 Reading Worksheet

Washington D.C.

Directions: Please answer the questions below after reading "Washington D.C."

1. What is the topic of the poem?

    a. George Washington

    b. Washington D.C

    c. monuments

2. What is Washington D. C.?

    a. city

    b. state

    c. nation's capital

3. What two men designed Washington D.C.?

    a. Abraham Lincoln and George Washington

    b. Pierre Charles L'Enfant and Benjamin Banneker

    c. Potomac and Virginia

4. List three places to visit in Washington D.C.

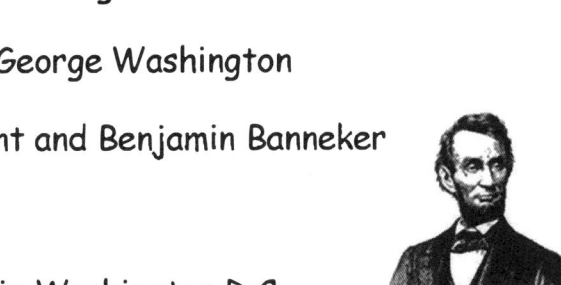

_____

_____

_____

16.4 - The Presidency

Name _____

16.4 Grammar Worksheet

Subject/Verb Agreement

Directions: Circle the correct verb in each sentence below.

1. Jim ___dive, dives___ off the coast of Florida.

2. Dolphins ___swim, swims___ around the water.

3. The scuba divers ___sink, sinks___ to the bottom of the water to look at the coral.

4. Everybody ___learn, learns___ about how to dive before going on the boat.

5. The ___captain, captains___ drives the boat to our diving area.

6. ___Instructor, Instructors___ help us put on our scuba diving outfits.

7. The captain or assistants ___tell, tells___ us when to come back to the boat.

8. The divers and captain ___share, shares___ stories of our journey.

9. Create a sentence with a singular subject and verb.
_____
_____

10. Create a sentence with a plural subject and verb.
_____
_____

16.4 - The Presidency

16.4 Writing Checklist

Name _____.

Informative Paragraph Checklist - *The Presidency*

Directions: Reread your writing carefully. Put a check in each box under Author as you complete each item.

Revise and Edit for the following:	Author
1. Clarity and Meaning **Ask yourself,** "Does the paragraph inform the reader about my chosen President?" "Do you have at least three facts about your President?" Rewrite parts that need revision.	

Revise and Edit for the following:	Author
2. Correct Use of Words **Ask yourself,** "Are specific details and words used?" "Are explanations used when needed?" "Do the sentences sound good together?" Rewrite parts that need revision.	

Revise and Edit for the following:	Author
3. Capitalization Use capitals at the beginning of each sentence and for every name. Make corrections if needed.	

Continue on the next page.

Revise and Edit for the following:	Author

4. Punctuation
    Use periods, exclamation points, and question marks.
    Use quotation marks for dialogue.
    Make corrections if needed.	

Revise and Edit for the following:	Author

5. Spelling
    Check for correct spelling.
    Make corrections if needed.	

Handwriting Practice 1

Name _____.

Handwriting - *The Presidency*

Directions:
Use the grey lines to help you write each letter on the first line.
Continue writing each letter on your own on the following lines.

Example

Example

Example

16.4 - The Presidency

255

Name _____

Spelling Test

Spelling - The Presidency

Directions:
As your teacher reads your words, write each spelling word on the blanks below.

1) _____   11) _____

2) _____   12) _____

3) _____   13) _____

4) _____   14) _____

5) _____   15) _____

6) _____   16) _____

7) _____   17) _____

8) _____   18) _____

9) _____   19) _____

10) _____ 20) _____

Name _____

Reading - *The Presidency*

Directions: Complete this worksheet after reading **"The President's Hats."** Include the major details to retell our story.

16.5 Reading Worksheet

The President's Hats

Main Idea: _____
_____
_____

Major Detail 1 ─────────────

Major Detail 2 ─────────────

Major Detail 3 ─────────────

Continue on the following page.

16.5 - The Presidency

Major Detail 4

Closing: _____
_____
_____
_____

16.5 Independent Reading

Name _____.

Reading - *The Presidency*

Directions: Read your independent reading book for 30 minutes. When you are done, write a short summary of what you have read.

I read _____ by _____
  (book title)   (author)

for 30 minutes today.

_____   _____
     My Signature   Parent/Guardian Signature

Write a short summary of what you read today.

_____ Details
_____
_____
_____
_____
_____
_____
_____

16.5 - The Presidency   259

Name _____.

Journal Entry - *Winter Holidays Around the World*

Directions: Write your response to the prompt on the lines below. Don't forget to check for complete sentences as you write.

Prompt: Describe a winter holiday that you celebrate? If you do not celebrate a winter holiday, discuss a winter holiday you would like to learn more about and why.

17.1 - Winter Holidays Around the World

Name _____

Spelling - *Winter Holidays Around the World*

17.2 Spelling Worksheet

Rainbow Words

Directions:
Please choose three different colored pencils. Write each spelling word three times using each color.

full _____   _____   _____

got _____   _____   _____

grow _____   _____   _____

hold _____   _____   _____

hot _____   _____   _____

hurt _____   _____   _____

if _____   _____   _____

keep _____   _____   _____

kind _____   _____   _____

laugh _____   _____   _____

light _____   _____   _____

long _____   _____   _____

Continue on the next page.

try   _____   _____   _____

warm   _____   _____   _____

way   _____   _____   _____

weigh   _____   _____   _____

symbol _____   _____   _____

cymbal _____   _____   _____

sun   _____   _____   _____

son   _____   _____   _____

Name _____.

Writing -
Winter Holidays Around the World
Directions:
Choose one holiday that you are interested in learning more about. After researching, complete the boxes to brainstorm your paragraph.

Structure of Paragraph Prewrite

Holiday: _____

Topic Sentence: _____

_____

Supporting Main Topic: Detail 1

Supporting Main Topic: Detail 2

Supporting Main Topic: Detail 3

Closing Sentence: _____

_____

17.2 - Winter Holidays Around the World

Name _____

Handwriting Practice 1

Handwriting - Winter Holidays Around the World

Directions:
Use the grey lines to help you write each letter on the first line. Continue writing each letter on your own on the following lines.

17.2 - Winter Holidays Around the World

Name _____.

17.3 Vocabulary Worksheet

Vocabulary Word Crossword - Winter Holidays Around the World

Directions: Use the definitions to complete the crossword puzzle using your vocabulary words.

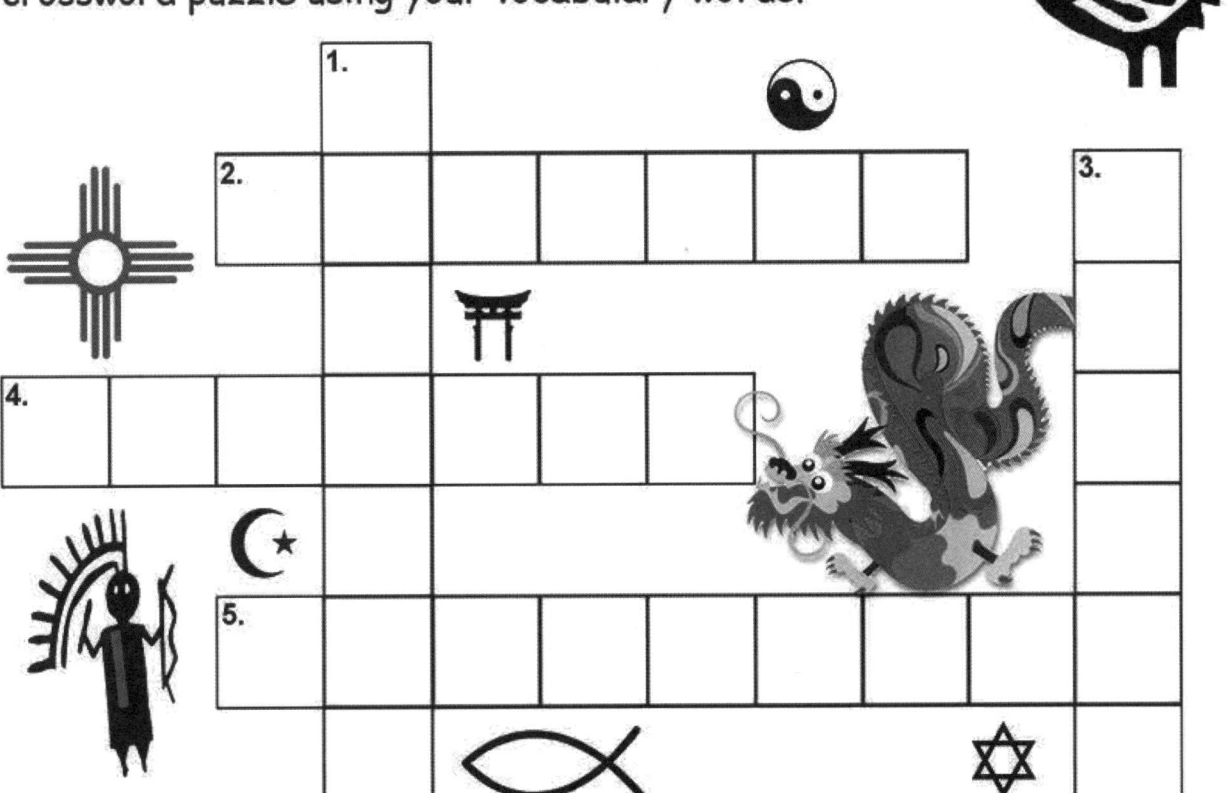

Across:
2. the usual practice of a person or group or the usual way of doing things
4. something that helps make time pass agreeably
5. the handing down of information, beliefs or customs from one generation to another
6. something that one thinks is true

Down:
1. the beliefs, social practices and characteristics of a racial, religious or social group
3. to put in order

17.3 - Winter Holidays Around the World   265

17.4 Spelling Worksheet

Name _____.

Fill in the Blanks - Winter Holidays Around the World

Directions: Fill in the blanks to spell each word.

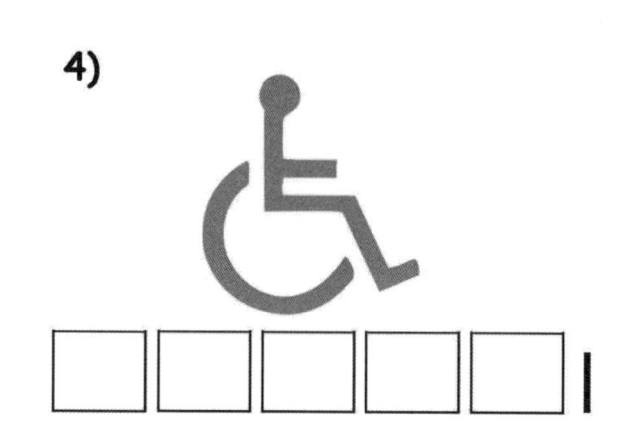

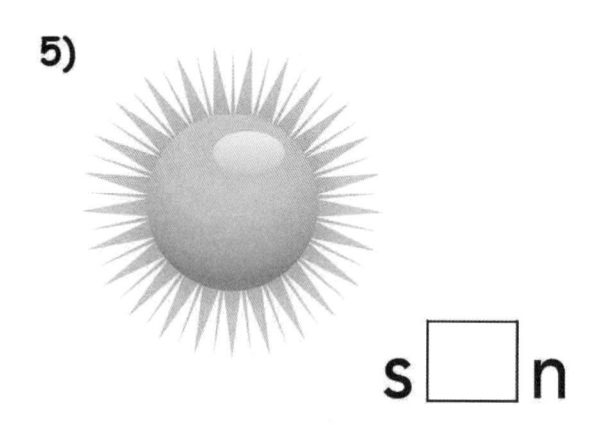

1) w ☐ ☐

2) w ☐ ☐ ☐ ☐

3) ☐ ☐ ☐ ☐ ☐ l

4) ☐ ☐ ☐ ☐ ☐ l

5) s ☐ n

6) s ☐ n

Continue on following page.

266   17.4 - Winter Holidays Around the World

Directions: Circle the correct spelling of the word and then write the correct spelling on the blank.

Circle Correct Spelling			Write Correct Word
1. ful	full	fulle	_____
2. got	gat	gawt	_____
3. grow	growe	groew	_____
4. hod	holde	hold	_____
5. hot	hout	hott	_____
6. hert	hurt	hurrt	_____
7. ife	iff	if	_____
8. kep	keep	kepe	_____
9. kind	kynd	kinde	_____
10. laf	laugh	lagh	_____
11. light	liht	liet	_____
12. logne	long	lawng	_____
13. try	tri	trie	_____
14. warme	werm	warm	_____

17.4 - Winter Holidays Around the World

Name _____

Reading

17.4 Reading Worksheet

Holidays Around the World

Directions: Please answer the questions below after reading "**Holidays Around the World.**" Circle the correct answer.

1. What do Christmas gifts help Christians remember?
    a. the date of Christmas
    b. when to go to church
    c. the gifts men brought to Jesus when he was born

2. Why does Hanukkah last eight days?
    a. the oil to burn the lamp lasted eight days
    b. because of the difference in the solar calendar and Jewish calendar
    c. children play with a dreidel for eight days

3. In the Chinese calendar, what is each year named after?
    a. a book
    b. an animal
    c. a sport

4. What are the Kwanzaa colors?
    a. green, black, and orange
    b. red, green, and blue
    c. red, black, and green

5. What is similar between Hanukkah and Diwali?
    _____
    _____
    _____

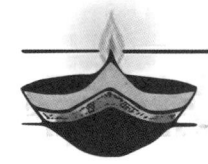

17.4 Grammar Worksheet

Name _____.

Subject/Verb Agreement Tenses -
Winter Holidays Around the World

Directions: Circle the correct verb in each sentence below. Make sure it is in the correct tense.

1. Present Tense:
   Gusty winds __roar, roars, will roar__ during the winter storm.

2. Past Tense:
   Snowflakes __dance, danced, will dance__ their way down to the ground.

3. Future Tense:
   I __play, played, will play__ in the snow this afternoon.

4. Present Tense:
   A holiday __allows, allow, will allow__ family and friends to share traditions.

5. Future Tense:
   My family and friends __will come, come, came__ to our holiday party.

6. Past Tense:
   The food __takes, took, will take__ up three tables at the holiday party.

Directions: Circle the subject. Underline the verb. Write **yes** or **no** if the subject determines the verb in each sentence.

7. We will build snowmen after the storm. _____

8. Max and Sue sled down the steepest hill. _____

9. They played outside until it became dark. _____

10. The ice skaters are going to skate on the frozen pond. _____

17.4 - Winter Holidays Around the World

17.4 Writing Checklist

Name _____.

Structure of Paragraph Checklist

Directions: Reread your writing carefully. Put a check in each box under **Author** as you complete each item.

Revise and Edit for the following:	Author
1. Clarity and Meaning **Ask yourself,** "Does the paragraph provide details about my chosen holiday?" "Are my details clear?" Rewrite parts that need revision.	

Revise and Edit for the following:	Author
2. Correct Use of Words **Ask yourself,** "Are specific details and words used?" "Are explanations used when needed?" "Do the sentences sound good together?"" Rewrite parts that need revision.	

Revise and Edit for the following:	Author
3. Capitalization Use capitals at the beginning of each sentence and for every name. Make corrections if needed.	

Continue on the next page.

Revise and Edit for the following:	Author

4. Punctuation
 	
   Use periods, exclamation points, and question marks.
 	
   Make corrections if needed.	

Revise and Edit for the following:	Author

5. Spelling
 	
   Check for correct spelling.
 	
   Make corrections if needed.	

Name _____

Handwriting -
Holidays Around the World
Directions:
Write each letter on the lines as shown.

Handwriting Practice 2

L

L

L

J

J

J

2

2

2

17.4 - Winter Holidays Around the World

Name _____

Spelling Test

Spelling –Winter Holidays Around the World

Directions:
As your teacher reads your words, write each spelling word on the blanks below.

1) _____	11) _____

2) _____	12) _____

3) _____	13) _____

4) _____	14) _____

5) _____	15) _____

6) _____	16) _____

7) _____	17) _____

8) _____	18) _____

9) _____	19) _____

10) _____	20) _____

17.5 - Winter Holidays Around the World

My name is _____

Reading - Winter Holidays Around the World

17.5 Reading Worksheet

Directions: Choose two holidays from our story "**Holidays Around the World**". Compare and contrast the holidays using the Venn Diagram below. Write the name of the holiday above the correct section. The middle section is for similarities.

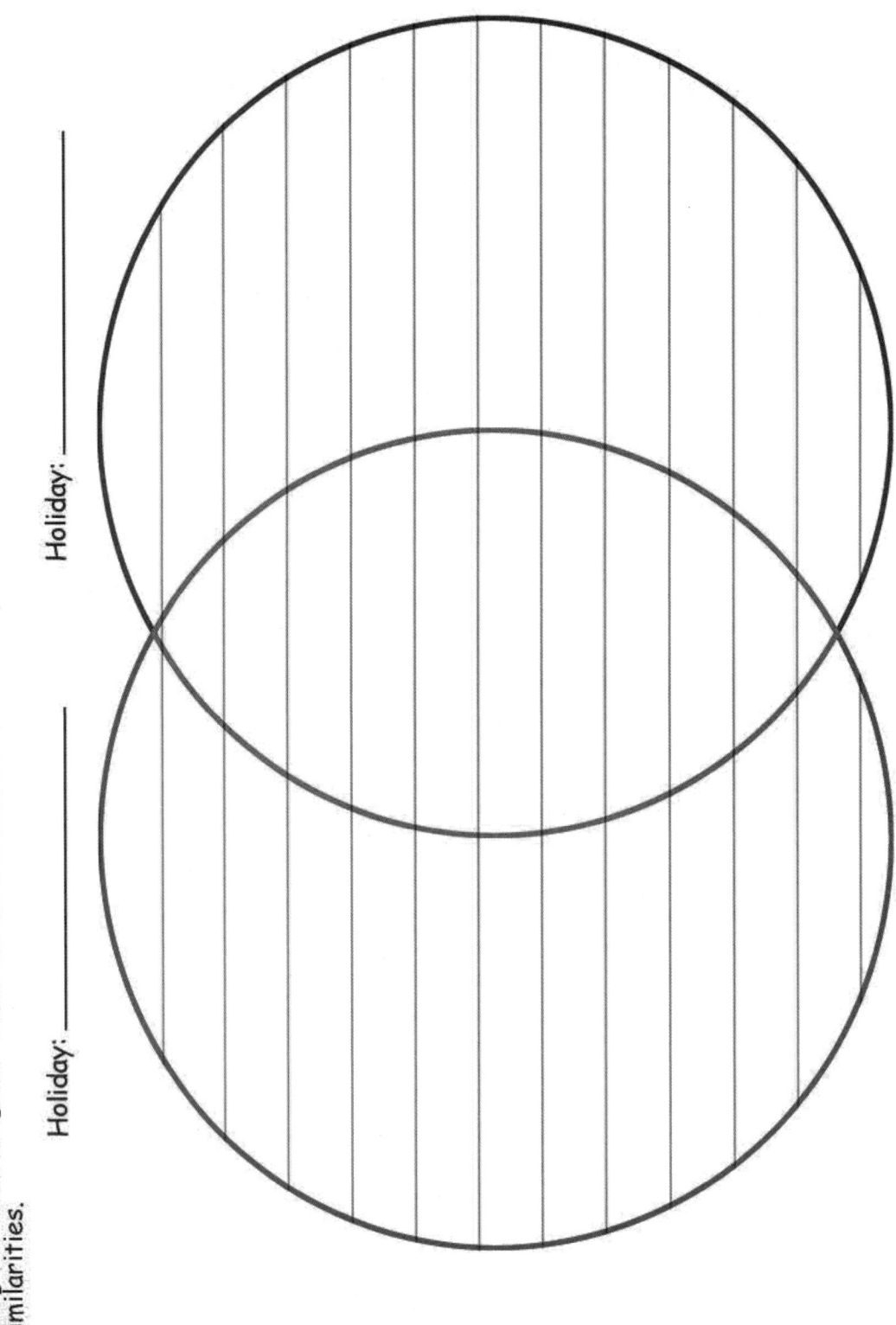

Holiday: _____

Holiday: _____

17.5 - Winter Holidays Around the World

17.5 Independent Reading

Name _____.

Reading - *Winter Holidays Around the World*

Directions: Read your independent reading book for 30 minutes. When you are done, write a short summary of what you have read on a sheet of lined paper.

I read _____ by _____
        (book title)   (author)

for 30 minutes today.

_____   _____
     My Signature   Parent/Guardian Signature

Compare and contrast what you have read today. You can compare/contrast characters or even topics.

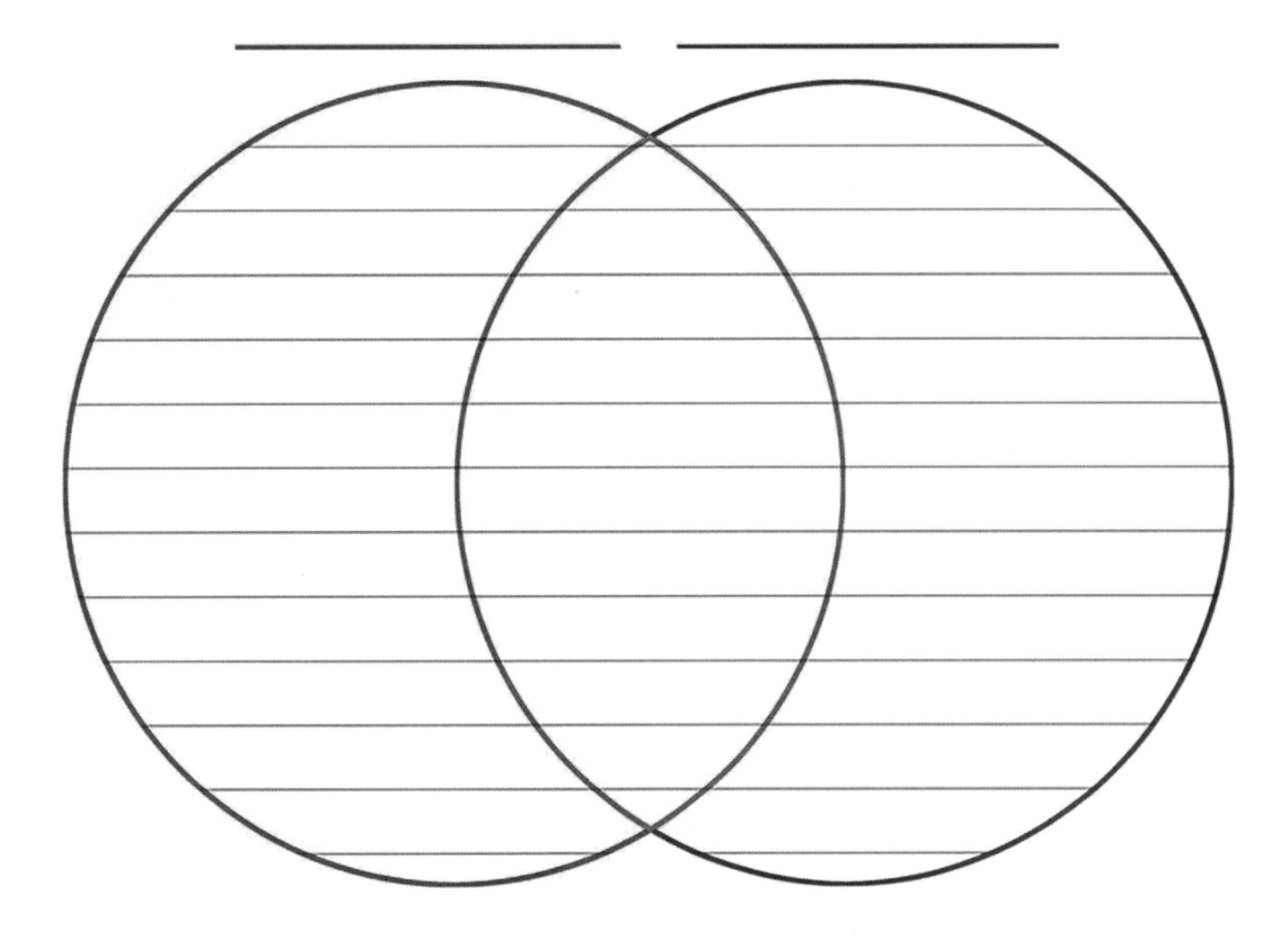

17.5 - Winter Holidays Around the World   275

Name _____.

Journal Entry - Time and New Years

Directions: Write your response to the prompt on the lines below. Don't forget to check for complete sentences as you write.

Prompt: How do you plan to celebrate the new year?

Name _____.

Spelling - *Time and New Years*

18.2 Spelling Worksheet

Rainbow Words

Directions:
Please choose three different colored pencils. Write each spelling word three times using each color.

much _____ _____ _____

myself _____ _____ _____

never _____ _____ _____

only _____ _____ _____

own _____ _____ _____

pick _____ _____ _____

seven _____ _____ _____

shall _____ _____ _____

show _____ _____ _____

six _____ _____ _____

small _____ _____ _____

start _____ _____ _____

Continue on the next page.

ten _____ _____ _____

today _____ _____ _____

tear _____ _____ _____

produce _____ _____ _____

wind _____ _____ _____

object _____ _____ _____

bass _____ _____ _____

desert _____ _____ _____

Name _____.

Writing - Time and New Years

Directions:
Write the resolution you created in the cause section. Brainstorm what may happen because of the resolution. Write these events in the effect boxes.

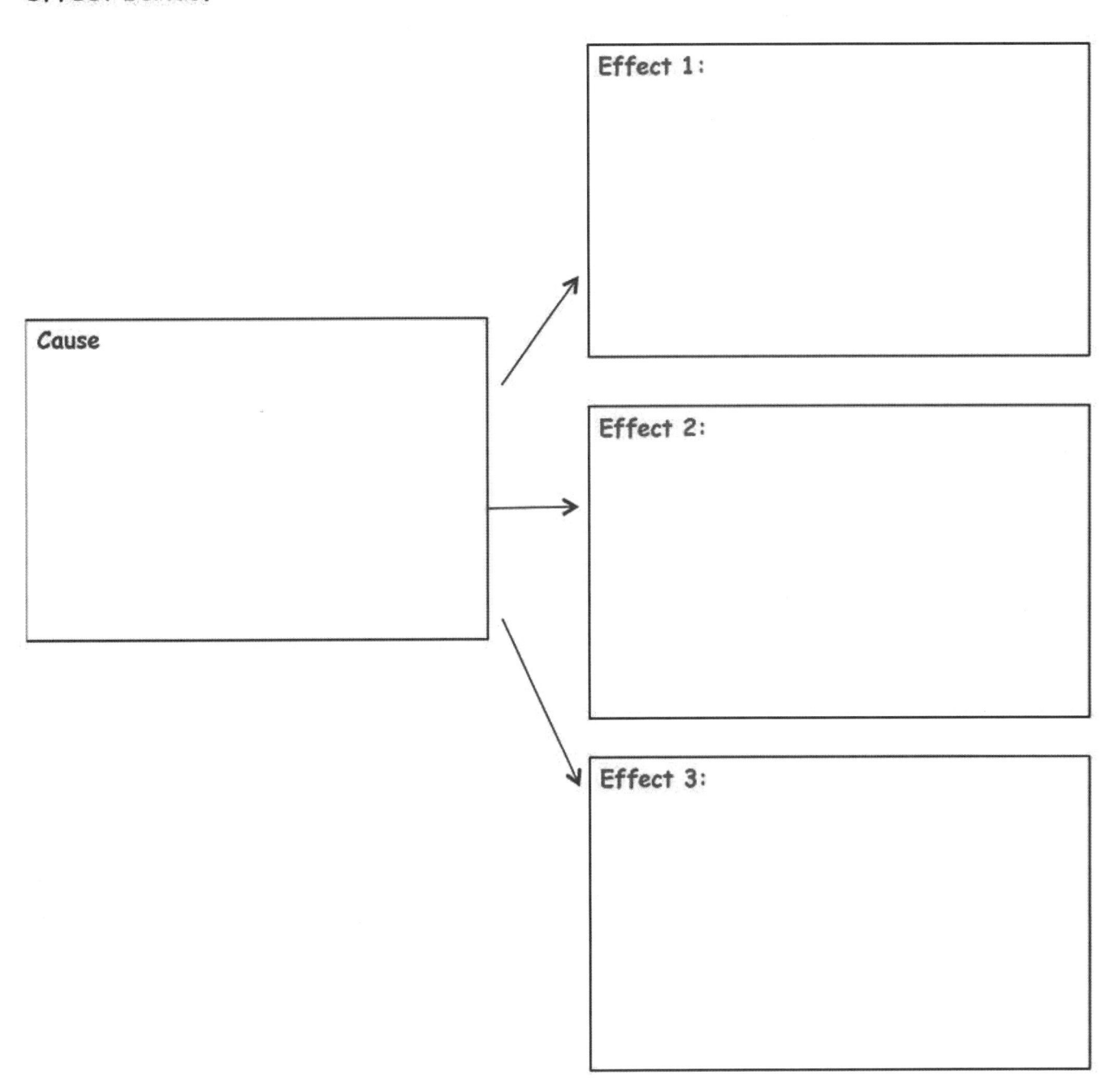

Cause and Effect Prewrite

Cause	Effect 1:
	Effect 2:
	Effect 3:

18.2 - Time and New Years

Handwriting Practice 1

Name _____

Handwriting - *Time and New Years*

Directions:
Use the grey lines to help you write each letter on the first line.
Continue writing each letter on your own on the following lines.

Example

Example

Example

Name _____.

Vocabulary Word Crossword

18.3 Vocabulary Worksheet

Directions: Use the definitions to complete the crossword puzzle using your vocabulary words.

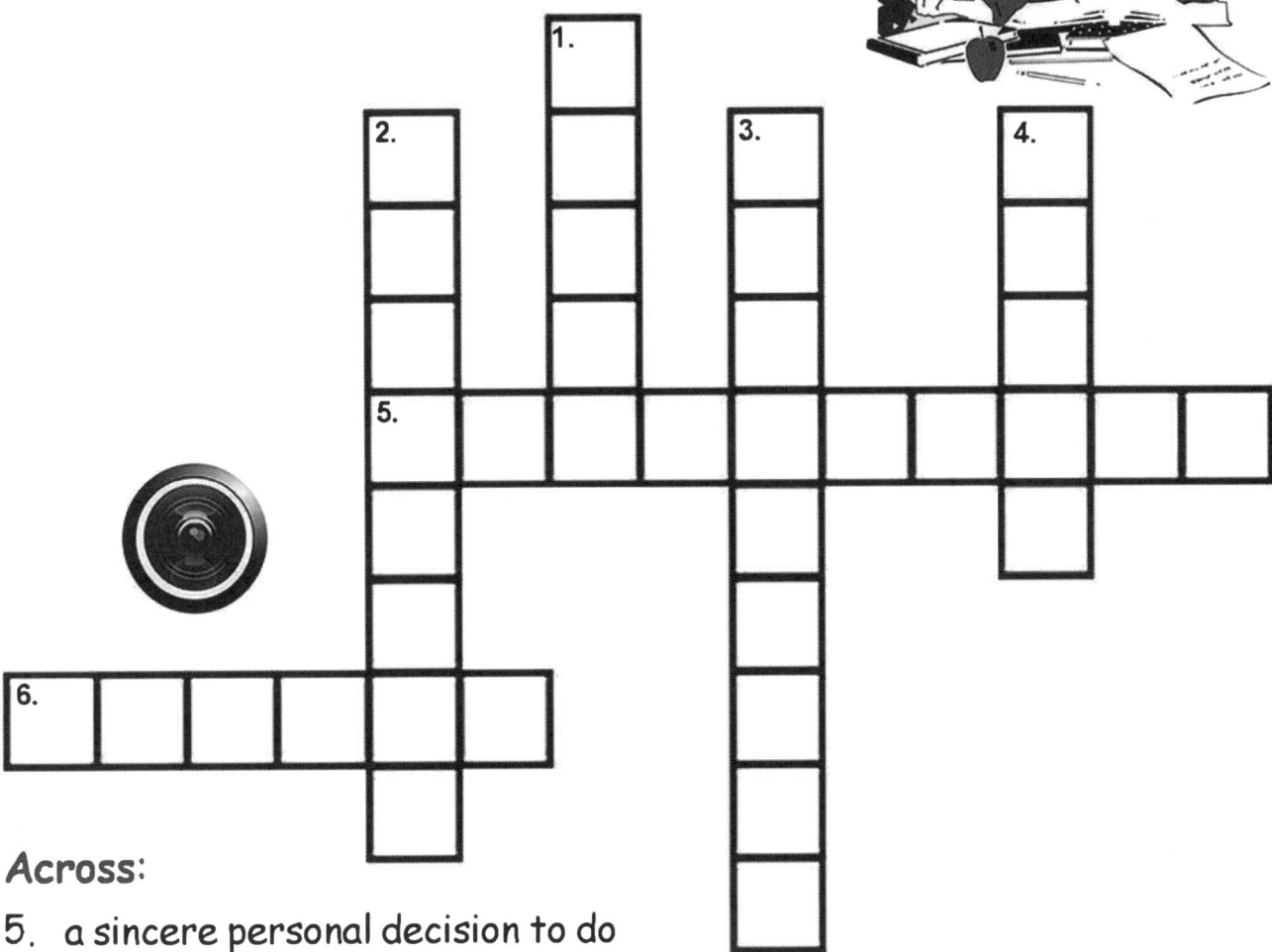

Across:

5. a sincere personal decision to do something
6. an opinion or suggestion offered about a decizion

Down:

1. a center of activity or interest
2. to begin to deal with
3. very impressive, bright, or smart
4. a way of behaving that has become fixed by being repeated often

18.3 - Time and New Years

281

Name _____

18.3 Grammar Worksheet

Diagram Subject and Verb -
Time and New Years

Directions: Write the subject on the first section of the line. Write the verb or predicate on the second section of each line. Identify if the subject is a noun or pronoun.

Example: My brother turned four years old yesterday.

              brother | turned

Subject: ___noun___

---

1. Susan bought the invitations for the party.

Subject: _____

2. They decorated the house with balloons and streamers.

Subject: _____

3. Springfield is the town for the party.

Subject: _____

282

18.3 - Time and New Years

18.4 Spelling Worksheet

Name _____.

Fill in the Blanks - *Time and New Years*

Directions: Fill in the blanks to spell each word.

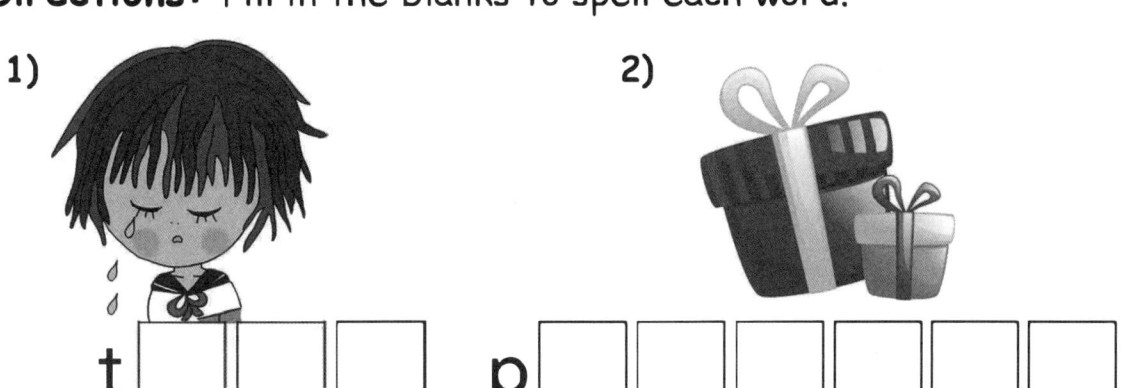

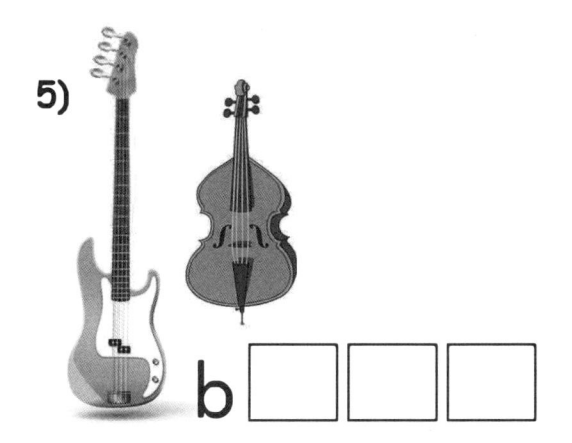

1) t ☐ ☐ ☐

2) p ☐ ☐ ☐ ☐ ☐ ☐

3) w ☐ ☐ ☐

4) o ☐ ☐ ☐ ☐ ☐

5) b ☐ ☐ ☐

6) d ☐ ☐ ☐ ☐ ☐

Continue on following page.

18.4 - Time and New Years　　　　　　283

Directions: Circle the correct spelling of the word and then write the correct spelling on the blank.

            Circle Correct Spelling   **Write Correct Word**

1. mutch   muche   much   _____
2. miself   myself   myselph   _____
3. nevr   naver   never   _____
4. only   onle   onely   _____
5. oun   own   owne   _____
6. pick   pik   pic   _____
7. sefen   seven   sevin   _____
8. shel   shal   shall   _____
9. show   showe   chowe   _____
10. siks   six   sics   _____
11. smaul   smal   small   _____
12. start   stert   stawrt   _____
13. tein   ten   tene   _____
14. todae   twoday   today   _____

18.4 Reading Worksheet

Oscar's New Year Plan

Name _____

Reading - *Time and New Years*

Directions: Please answer the question below after reading "**Oscar's New Year Plan.**" Circle the correct answer.

1. How late did Oscar stay up to ring in the New Year?
    a. until midnight
    b. until noon
    c. until 8 o'clock

2. What resolution did Sasha choose?
    a. exercise
    b. watch less TV
    c. eat healthier

3. What advice did mom give Oscar about his resolutions?
    a. choose an easier resolution
    b. choose one resolution
    c. do not pick a resolution

4. How did Oscar use the advice his mom gave him?

_____
_____
_____
_____
_____

18.4 - Time and New Years

Name _____

Nouns, Pronouns and Verbs -
Time and New Years

18.4 Grammar Worksheet

Directions: Complete the paragraph. Write a word or word phrase using the direction in parenthesis.

_____ (*pronoun*) went to visit my _____ (*noun-person*)

in _____ (*proper noun-place*). While visiting, everyone

_____ (*past tense verb*) to the zoo and _____

(*common noun-place*). _____ (*pronoun*) favorite thing to do was

_____ (*verb*) the _____ (*noun*). I hope

_____ (*pronoun*) can _____ (*verb*)

again next year!

Directions: Look at the underlined word in the sentence. Write whether it is a noun, pronoun or verb.

1. Winter is my favorite <u>season</u> of the year. _____

2. <u>Did</u> you <u>see</u> the firework show last year? _____

3. I hope <u>they</u> can make it to the holiday party. _____

4. Please <u>mail</u> the invitations. _____

5. The <u>mail</u> is sitting on the table. _____

18.4 Writing Checklist

Name _____.

Cause and Effect Paragraph Checklist

Directions: Reread your writing carefully. Put a check in each box under **Author** as you complete each item. Once all the boxes are checked, your **peer partner** will check your paragraph and put a check in each box.

Revise and Edit for the following:	Author	Peer Partner
1. Clarity and Meaning *Ask yourself,* "Does the paragraph state your resolution and the effects of it?" "Are the effects clear?" Rewrite parts that need revision.		

Revise and Edit for the following:	Author	Peer Partner
2. Correct Use of Words *Ask yourself,* "Are specific details and words used?" "Are explanations used when needed?" "Do the sentences sound good together?" Rewrite parts that need revision.		

Revise and Edit for the following:	Author	Peer Partner
3. Capitalization Use capitals at the beginning of each sentence and for every name. Make corrections if needed.		

Continue on the next page.

18.4 - Time and New Years

Revise and Edit for the following:	Author	Peer Partner

4. Punctuation
 	
    Use periods, exclamation points and question marks.
 	
    Use quotation marks for dialogue.
 	
    Make corrections if needed.		

Revise and Edit for the following:	Author	Peer Partner

5. Spelling
 	
    Check for correct spelling.
 	
    Make corrections if needed.		

Handwriting Practice 2

Name _____.

Handwriting - *Time and New Years*

Directions:
Use the grey lines to help you write each letter on the first line. Continue writing each letter on your own on the following lines.

Example

D D D D D D D D

D

D

D

L

L

L

G

G

G

18.4 - Time and New Years 289

Name _____

Spelling Test

Spelling - *Time and New Years*

Directions:
As your teacher reads your words, write each spelling word on the blanks below.

1) _____   11) _____

2) _____   12) _____

3) _____   13) _____

4) _____   14) _____

5) _____   15) _____

6) _____   16) _____

7) _____   17) _____

8) _____   18) _____

9) _____   19) _____

10) _____   20) _____

Name _____

Cause and Effect -
Time and New Years

Directions:
Write the missing cause or effect from "Oscar's New Year Plan" in the graphic organizer below.

18.5 Reading Worksheet

Oscar's New Year Plan

Cause		Effect
	→	Oscar yawned. He is tired.
Oscar watched television over Caleb's shoulder. His resolution was to not watch television.	→	
Mom gave Oscar advice to pick one resolution.	→	

18.5 - Time and New Years

291

18.5 Independent Reading

Name _____

Reading - *Time and New Years*

Directions: Read your independent reading book for 30 minutes. When you are done, write a short summary of what you have read.

I read _____ by _____
(book title)   (author)

for 30 minutes today.

_____   _____
My Signature   Parent/Guardian Signature

Directions: Find examples of cause and effect in your reading today. Write a description of the cause and effect in the graphic organizer below.

Cause   **Effect**

18.5 - Time and New Years

Weekly Sight Words

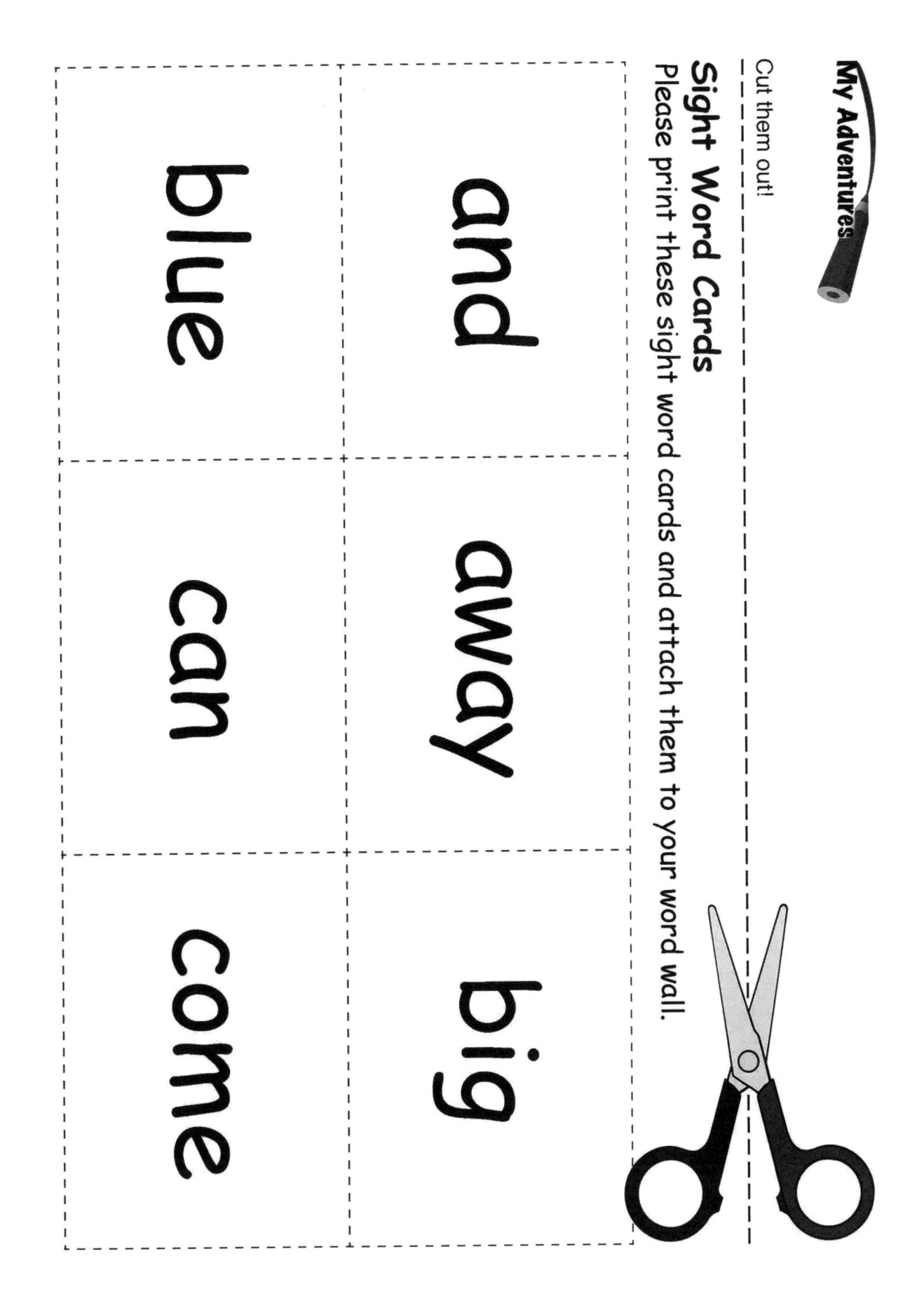

Cut them out!

Sight Word Cards
Please print these sight word cards and attach them to your word wall.

and	away	big
blue	can	come

Continue on next page.

1.1 - My Adventures

down	funny
find	go
for	

Space Adventures

Sight Word Cards

Here are your sight words for lesson 2.1. Cut out these flashcards along the dotted lines. Add these to your word wall.

Cut them out!

help	here	I
in	is	it

Continue on next page.

2.1 - Space Adventures

jump	make
little	me
look	my

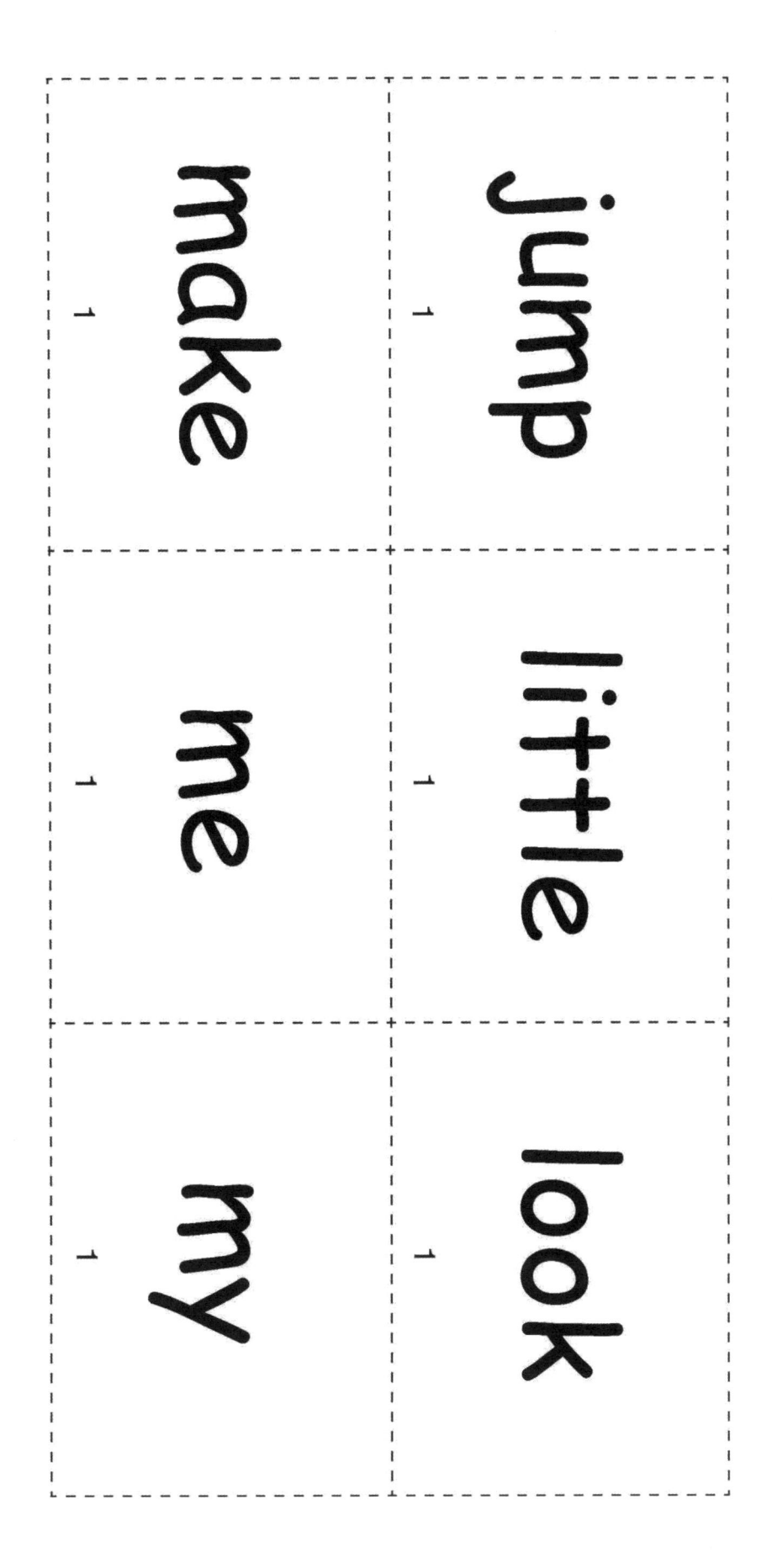

2.1 - Space Adventures

Ocean Adventures

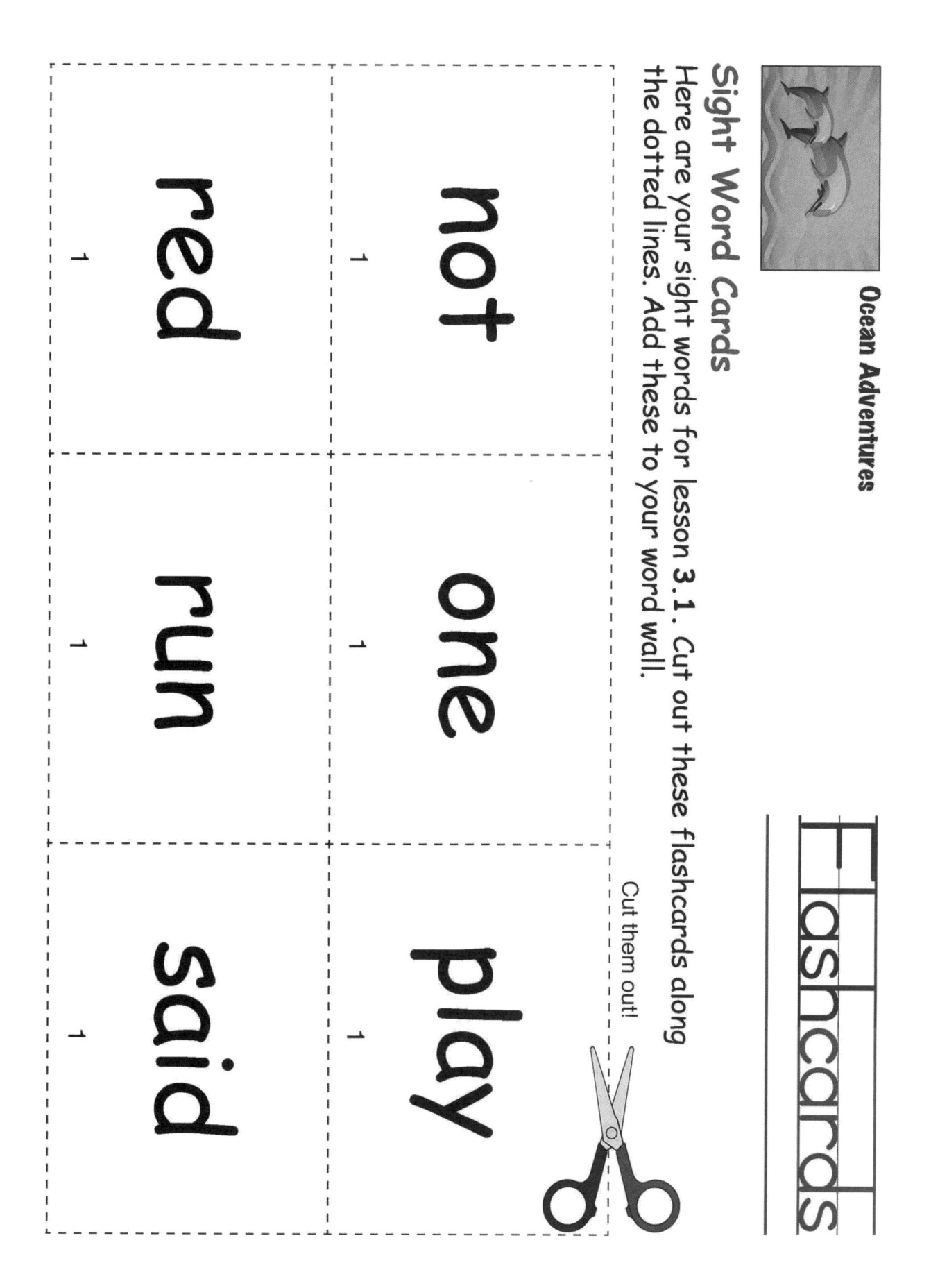

Sight Word Cards

Here are your sight words for lesson **3.1**. Cut out these flashcards along the dotted lines. Add these to your word wall.

Flashcards

not	one	play
1	1	1
red	run	said
1	1	1

Cut them out!

Continue on next page.

3.1 - Ocean Adventures

see	the	three
to	two	up

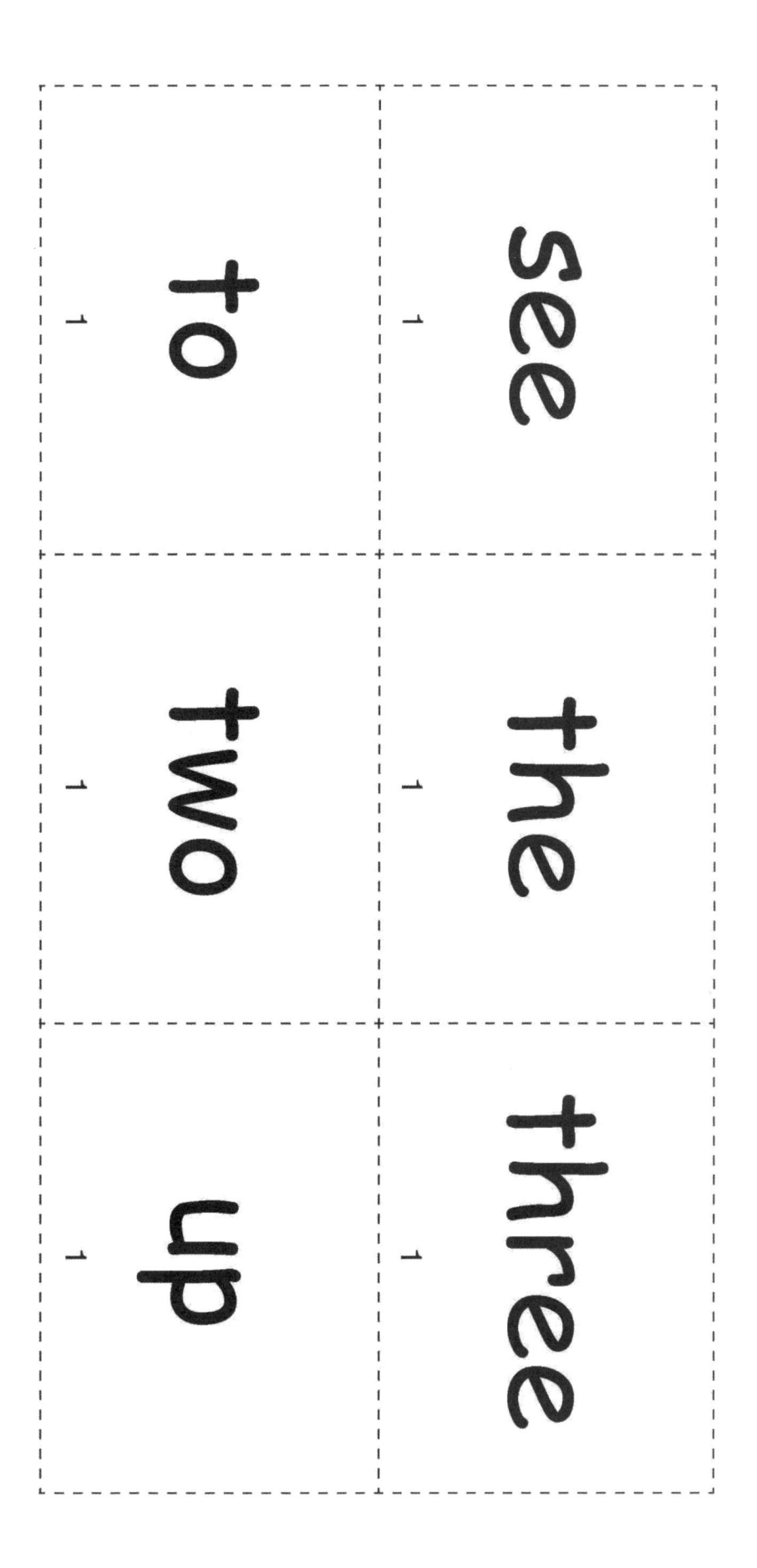

3.1 - Ocean Adventures

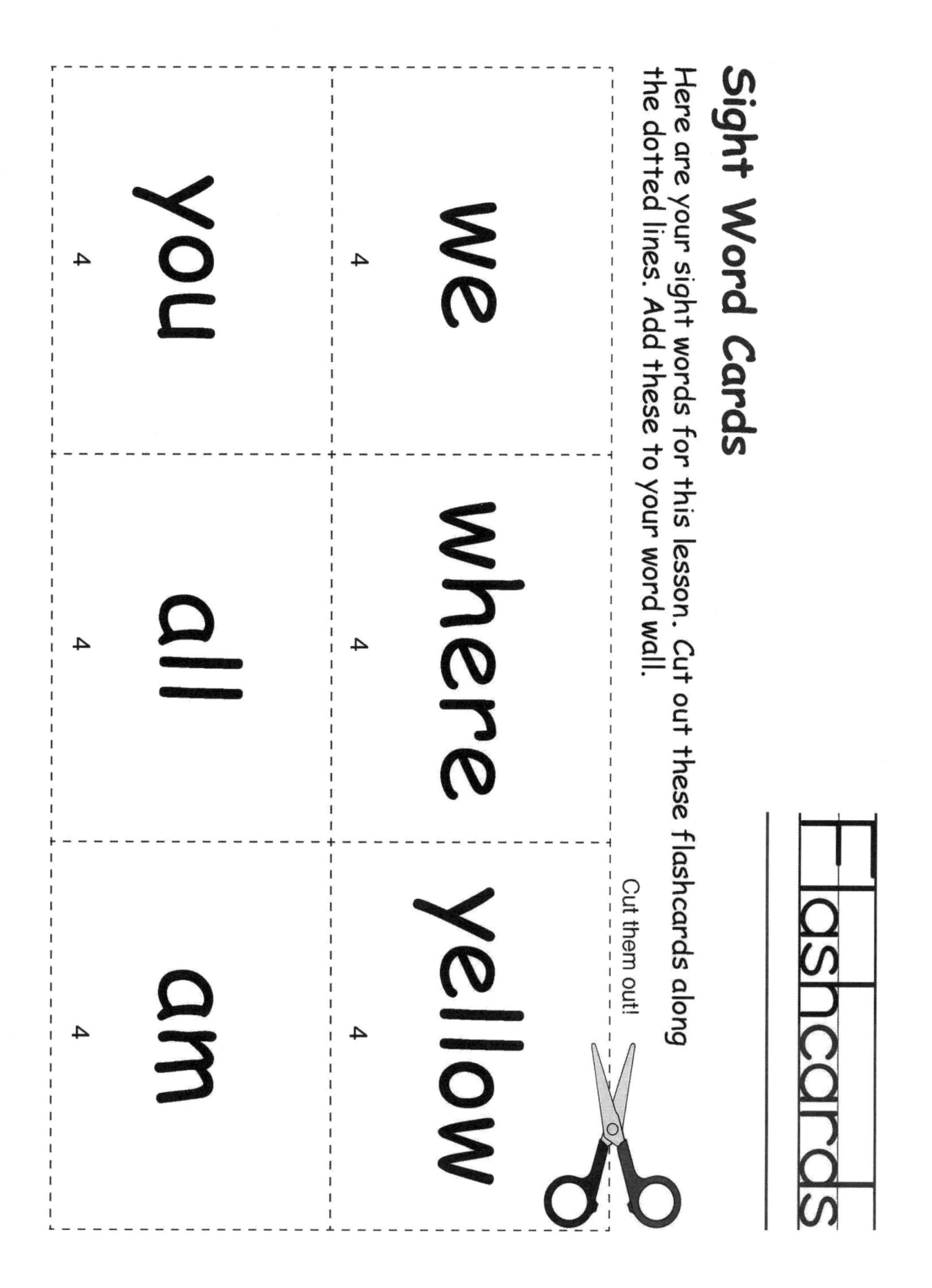

Sight Word Cards

Here are your sight words for this lesson. Cut out these flashcards along the dotted lines. Add these to your word wall.

Flashcards

Cut them out!

we	where	yellow
you	all	am

Continue on next page.

4.1 - Fables

are	be
at	black
ate	

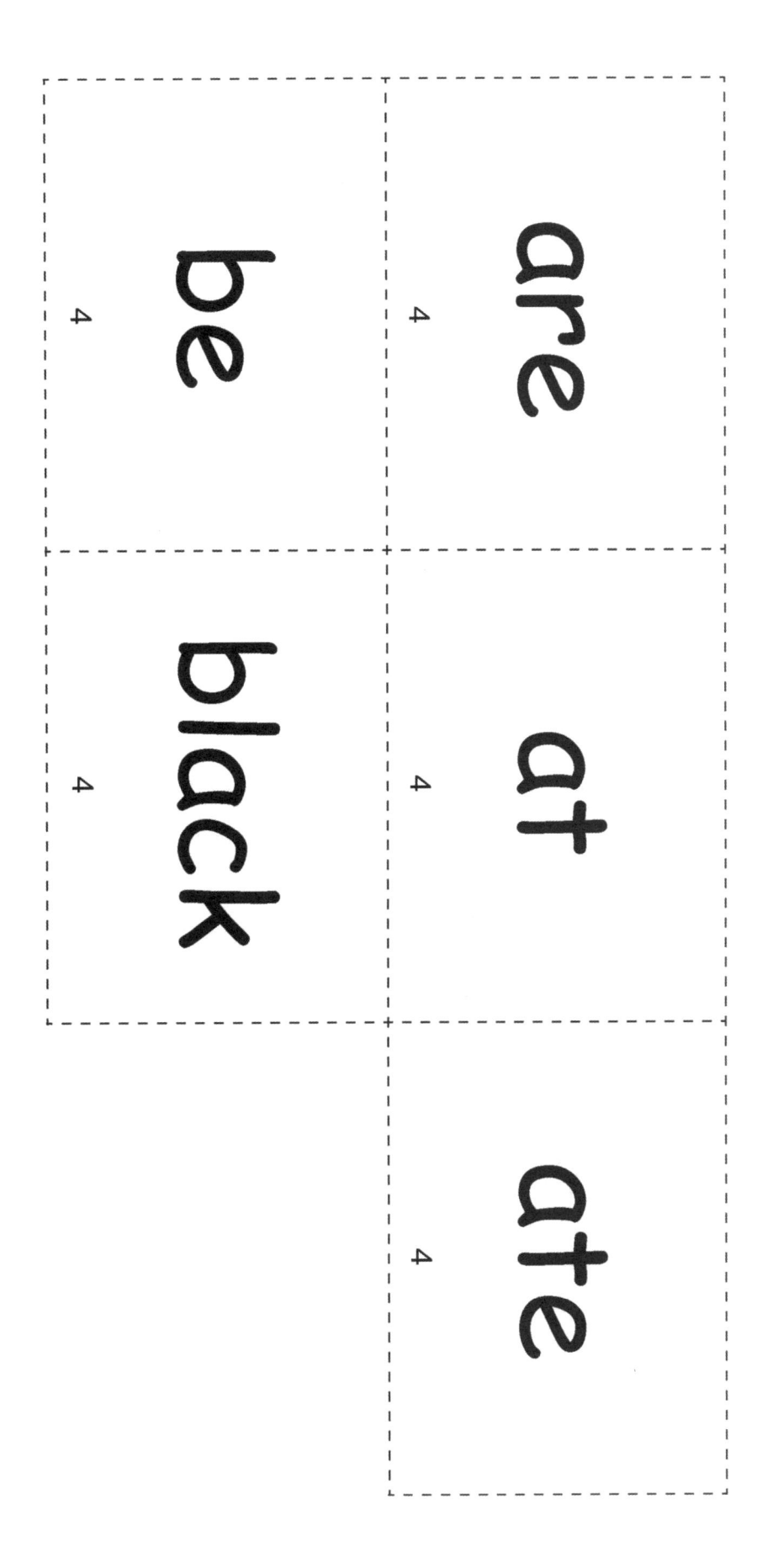

4.1 - Fables

Sight Word Cards

Here are your sight words for the week. Cut out these flashcards along the dotted lines. Add these to your word wall.

Flashcards

Cut them out!

brown	but	came
did	do	eat

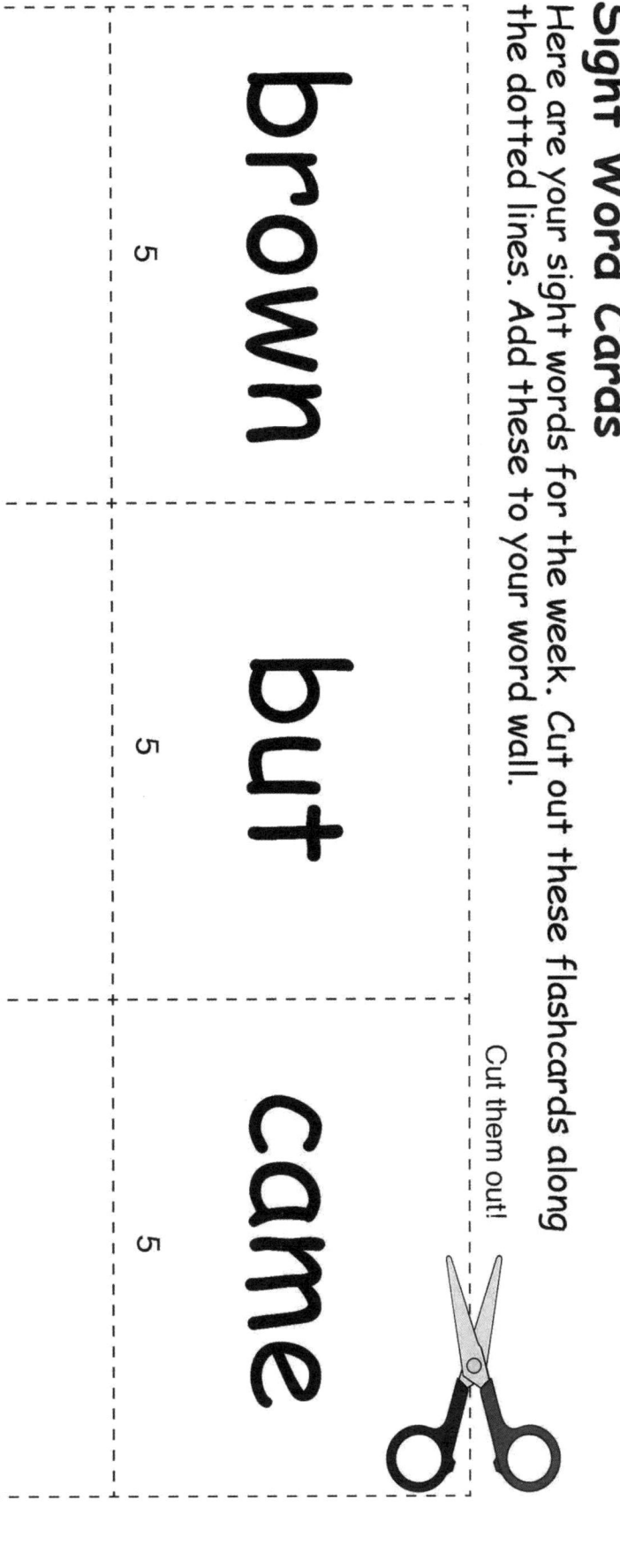

Continue on the next page.

5.1 - Myths

four	have
get	he
good	into

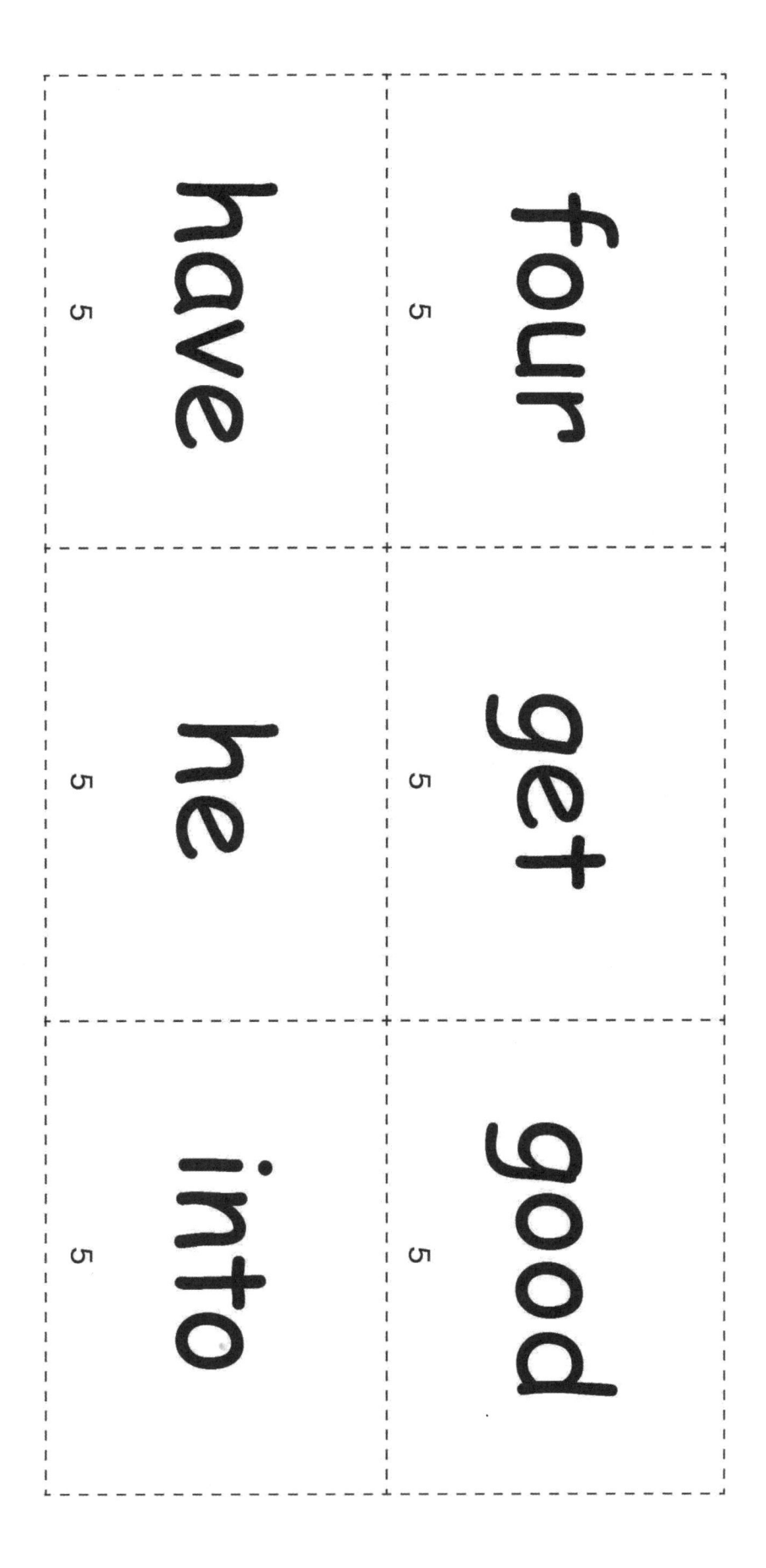

Spelling - *Why Tales*

Cut them out!

Sight Word Cards
Please print these sight word cards and attach them to your word wall.

like	must	new
no	now	on

Continue on the next page.

pretty	our
ran	out
ride	please

Spelling - *Solving Problems*

Sight Word Cards

Here are your sight words for the week. Cut out these flashcards along the dotted lines. Add these to your word wall.

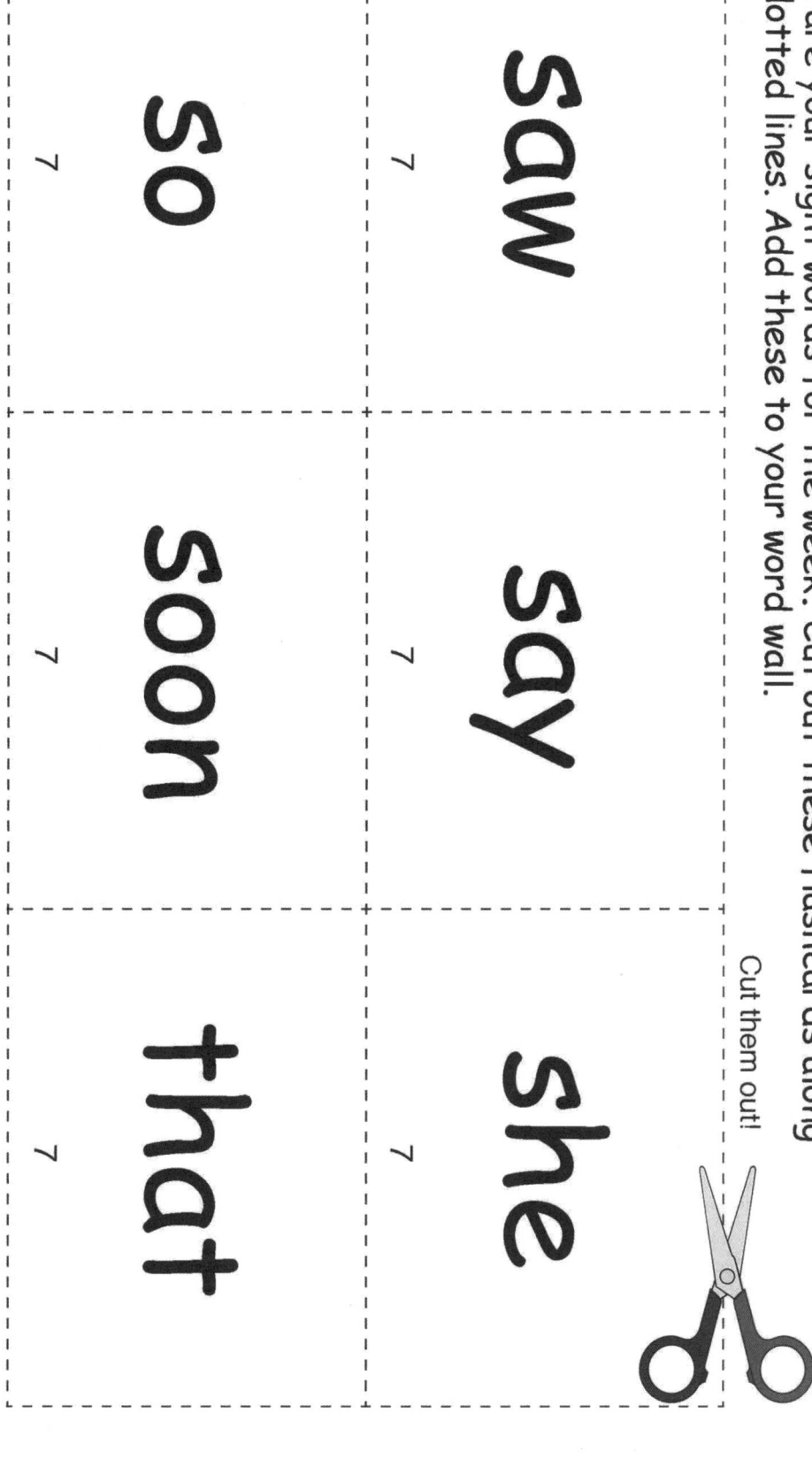

saw	say	she
so	soon	that

Cut them out!

Continue on the next page.

7.1 - Solving Problems

there	too
they	under
this	want

7.1 - Solving Problems

Sight Words - *Asking Questions*

Sight Word Cards

Here are your sight words for this lesson. Cut out these flashcards along the dotted lines. Add these to your word wall.

Cut them out!

Flashcards

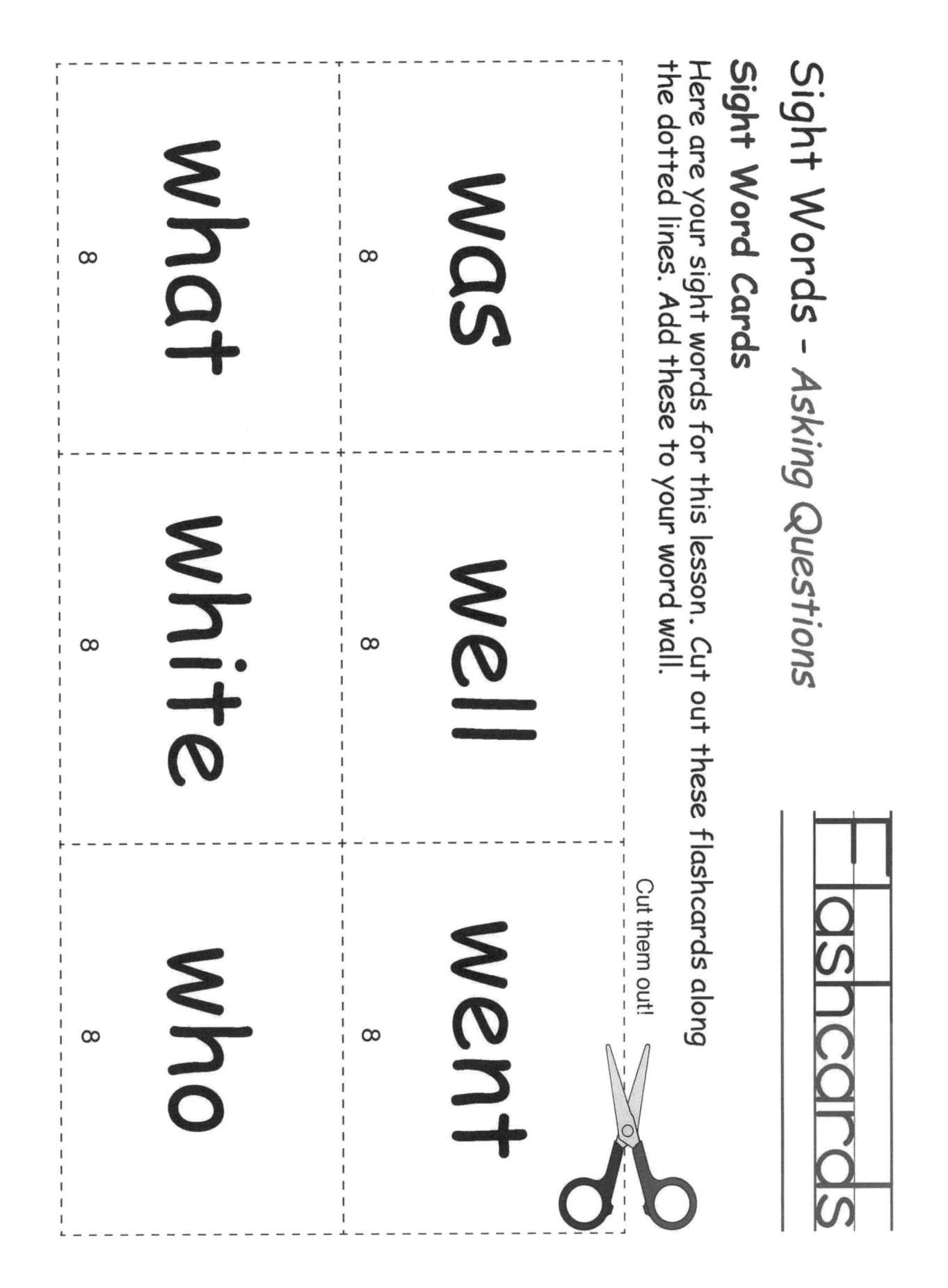

was	well	went
what	white	who

Continue on next page.

8.1 - Asking Questions

will	after
with	again
yes	an

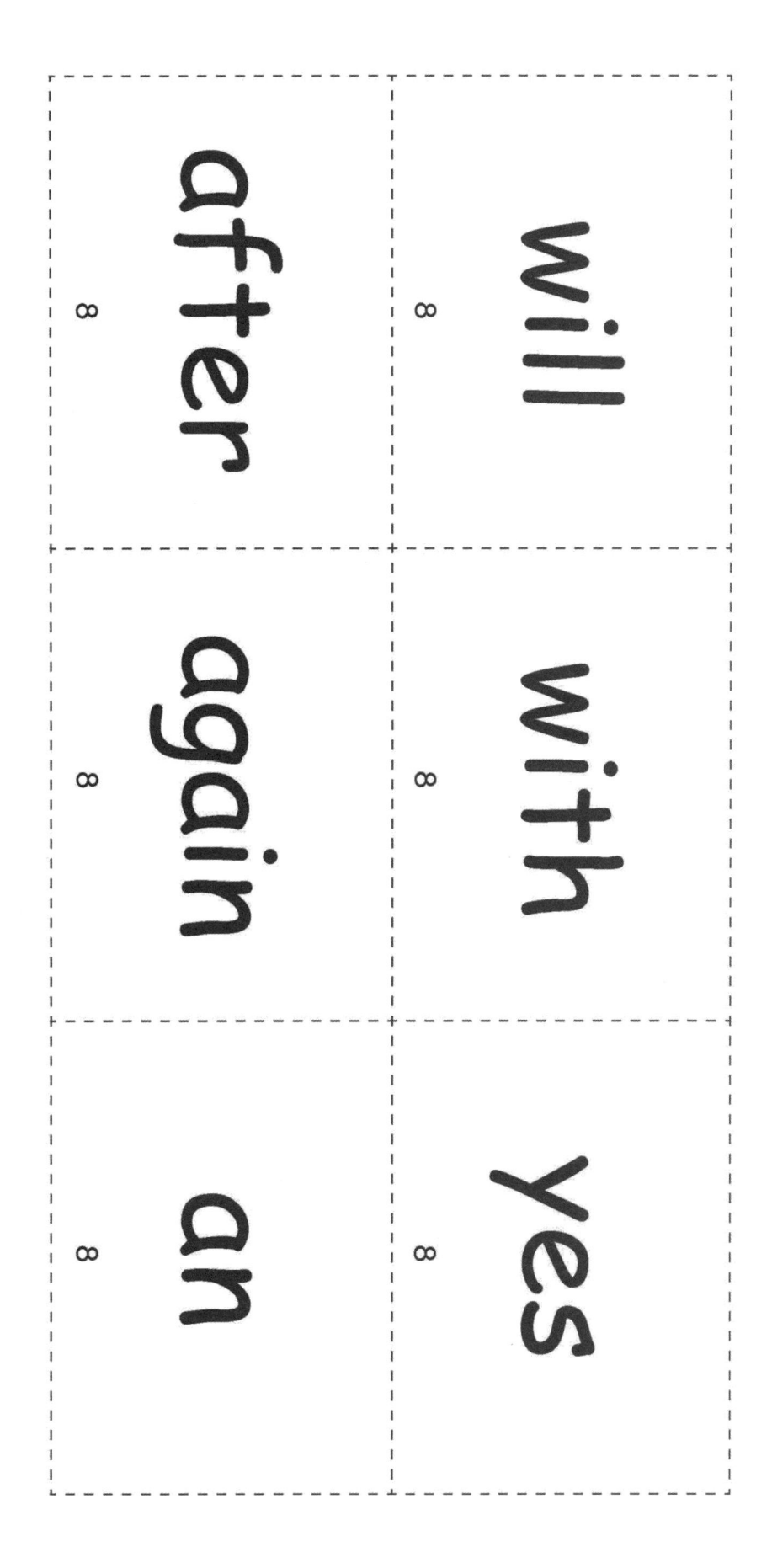

8.1 - Asking Questions

Sight Words - Inventions

Sight Word Cards

Here are your sight words for this lesson. Cut out these flashcards along the dotted lines. Add these to your word wall.

Flashcards

Cut them out!

any	as	ask
by	could	every

Continue on the following page.

fly	going
from	had
give	has

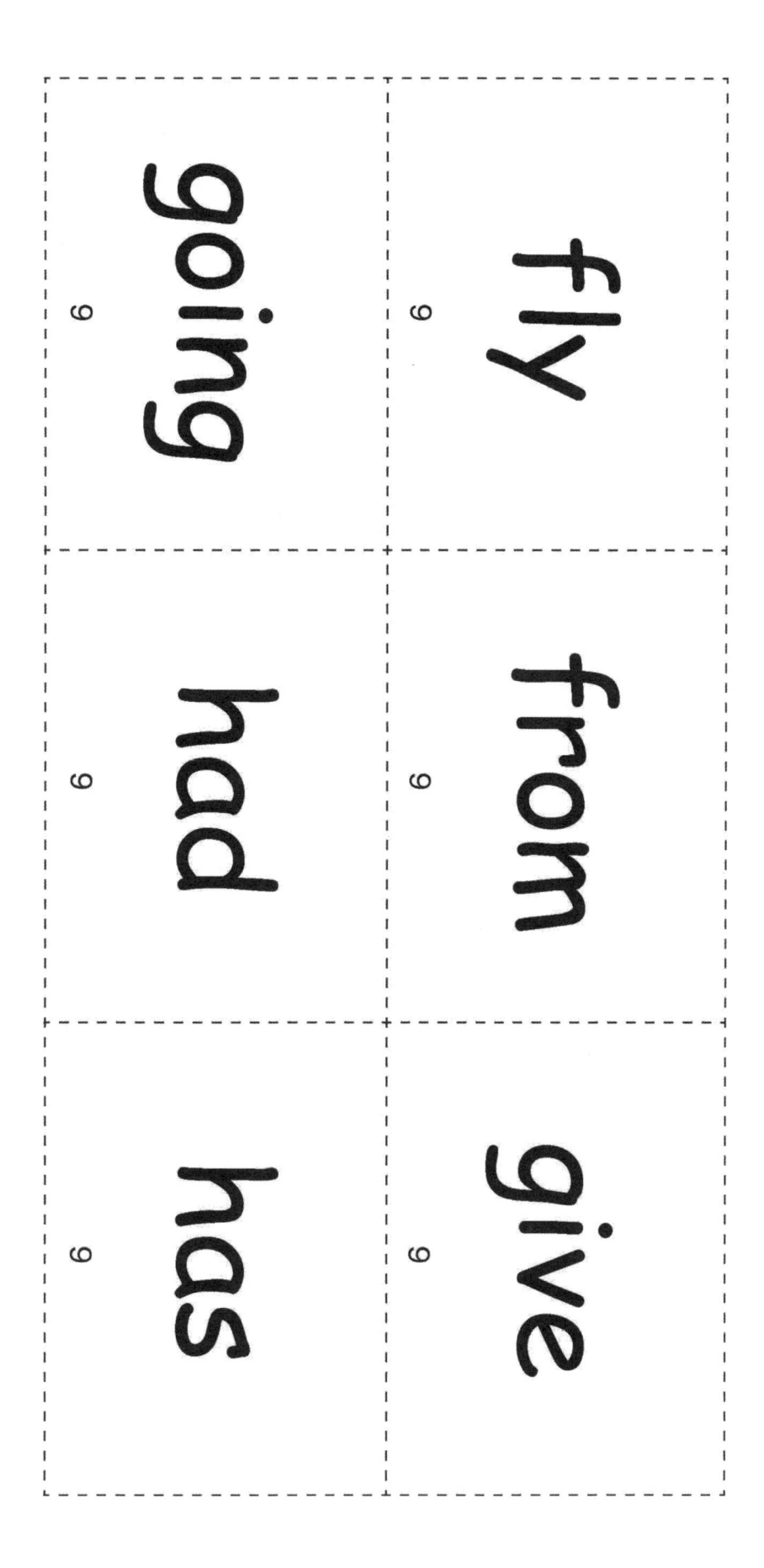

Sight Words - *Pond Animals*

Sight Word Cards

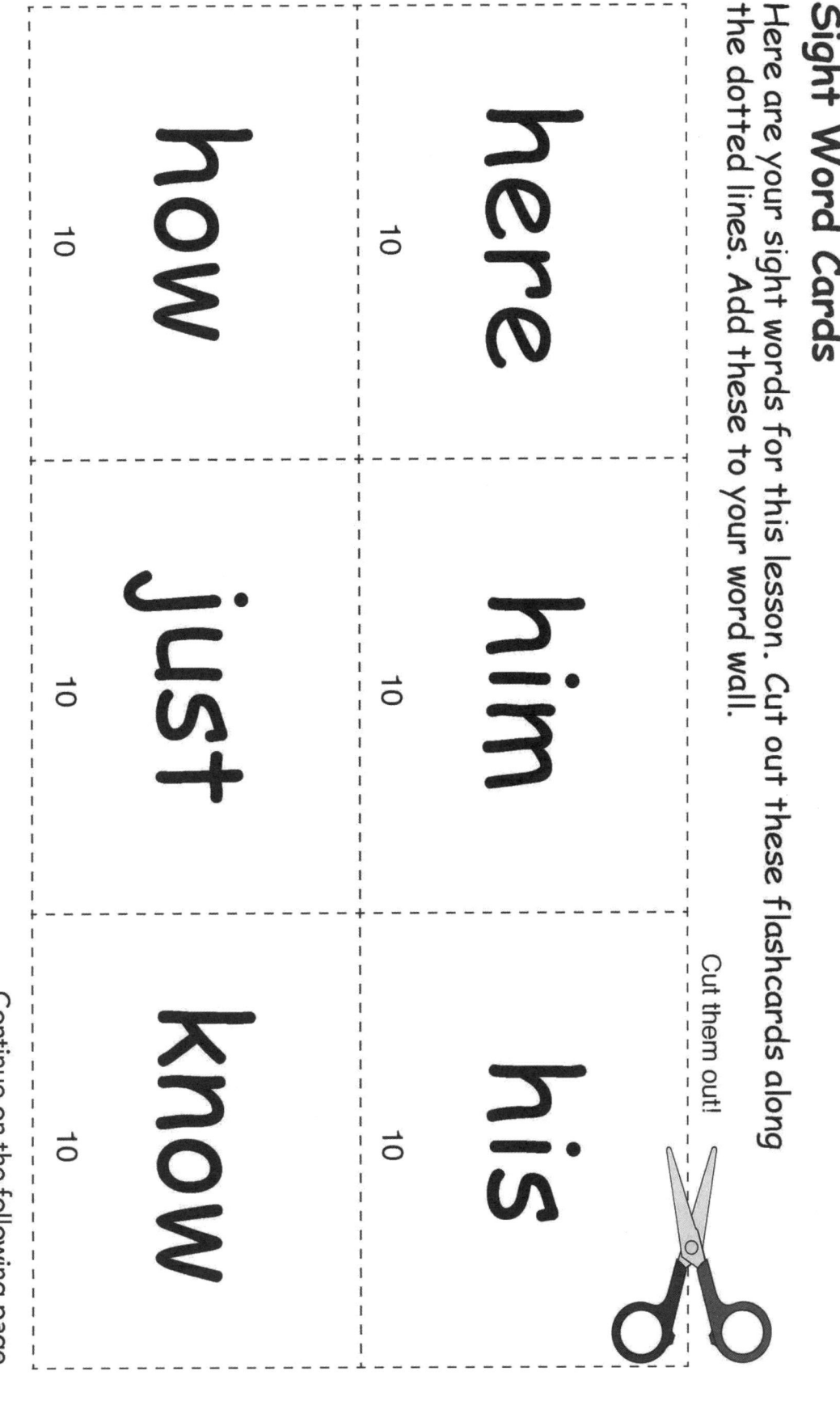

Here are your sight words for this lesson. Cut out these flashcards along the dotted lines. Add these to your word wall.

Cut them out!

here	him	his
10	10	10
how	just	know
10	10	10

Continue on the following page.

Flashcards

let	live	may
of	old	once

10.1 - Pond Animals

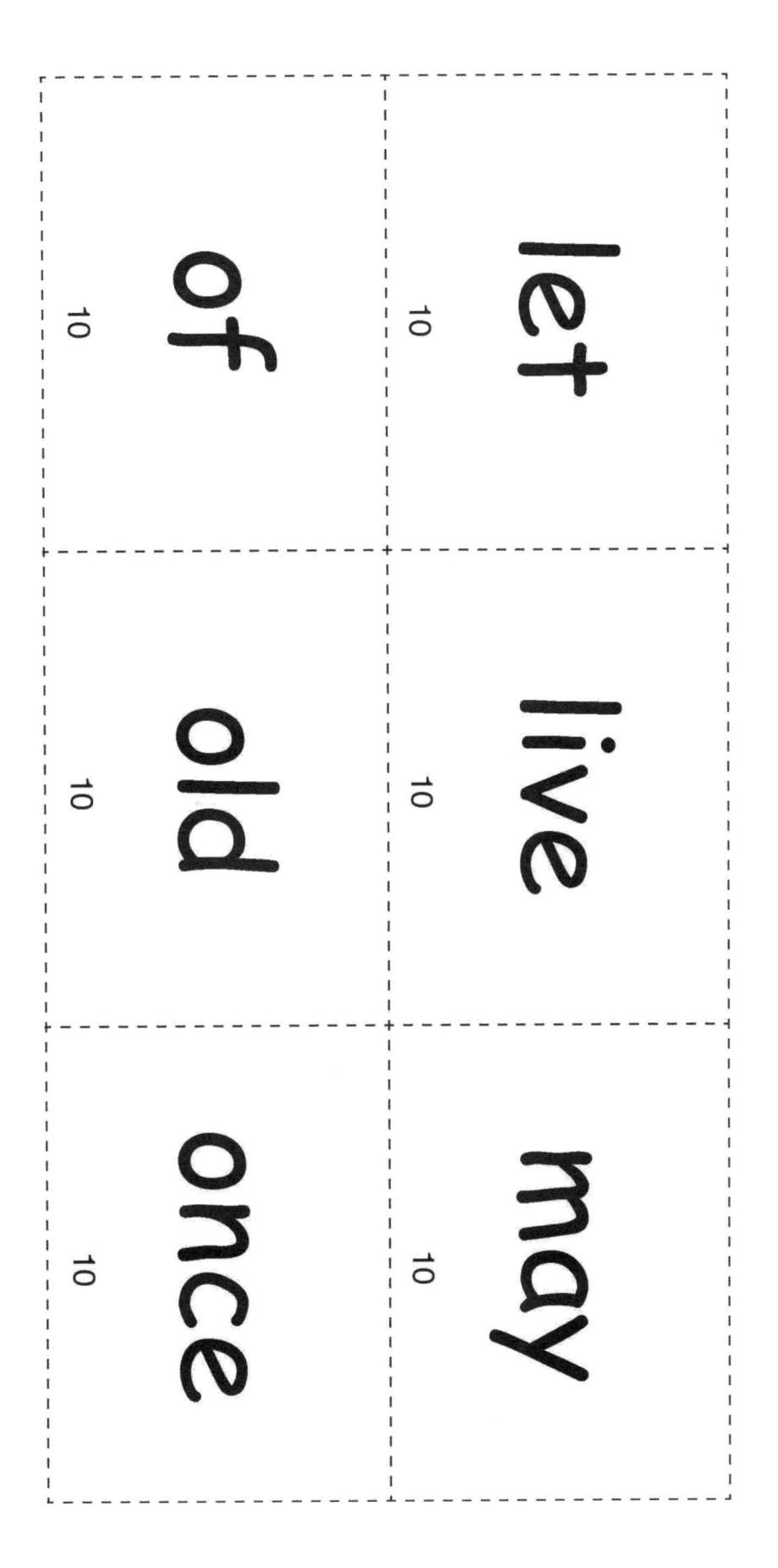

Sight Words - *Animal Friends*

Sight Word Cards

Here are your sight words for this lesson. Cut out these flashcards along the dotted lines. Add these to your word wall.

Cut them out!

open	over	round
11	11	11

some	stop	thank
11	11	11

Continue on the following page.

11.1 - Animal Friends

them

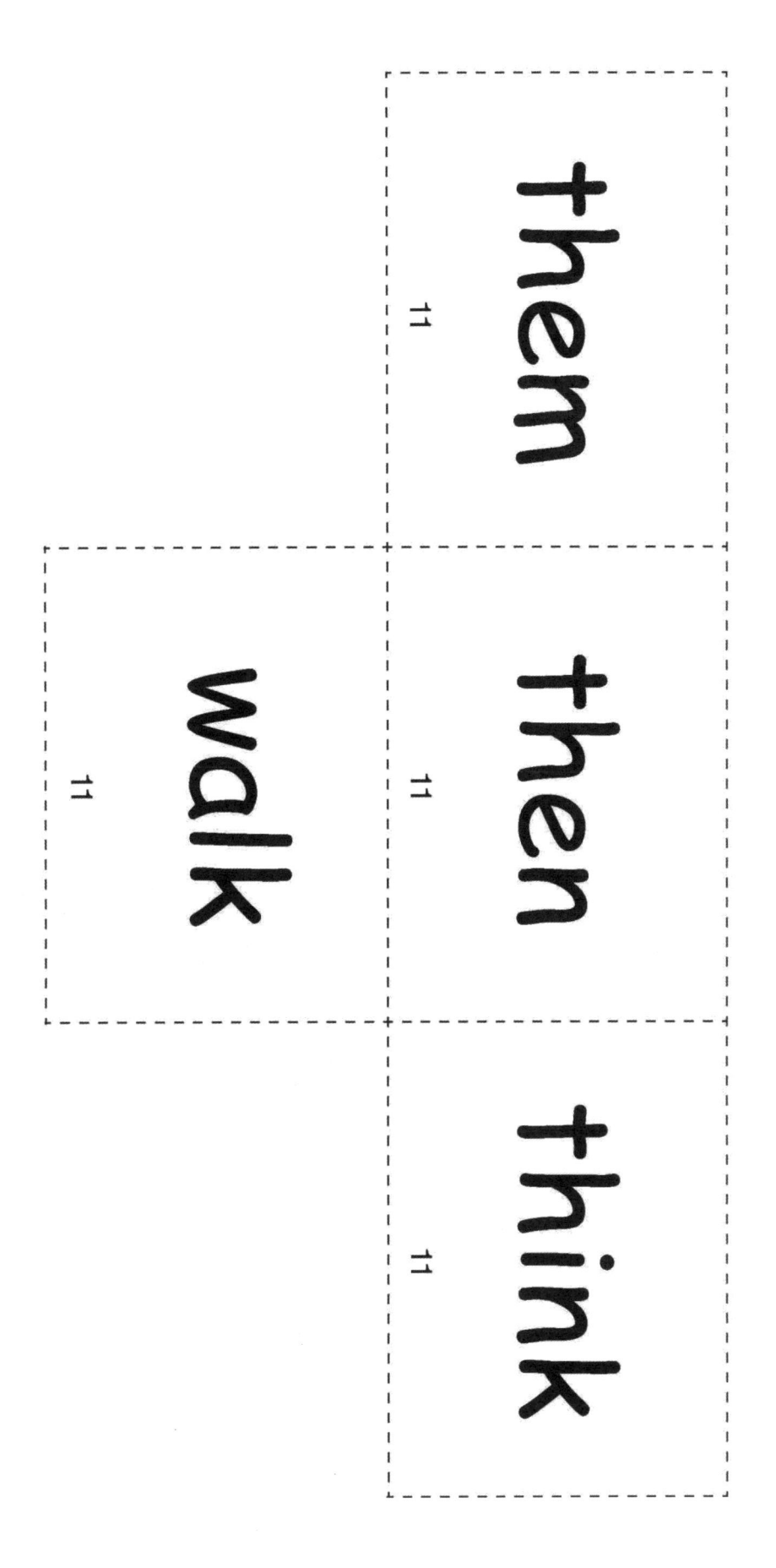

then

walk

think

11.1 - Animal Friends

Sight Words - *Night Animals*

Sight Word Cards

Here are your sight words for this lesson. Cut out these flashcards along the dotted lines. Add these to your word wall.

Cut them out!

Flashcards

were	when	always
12	12	12

around	because	been
12	12	12

Continue on the following page.

12.1 - Night Animals

before	buy
best	call
both	cold

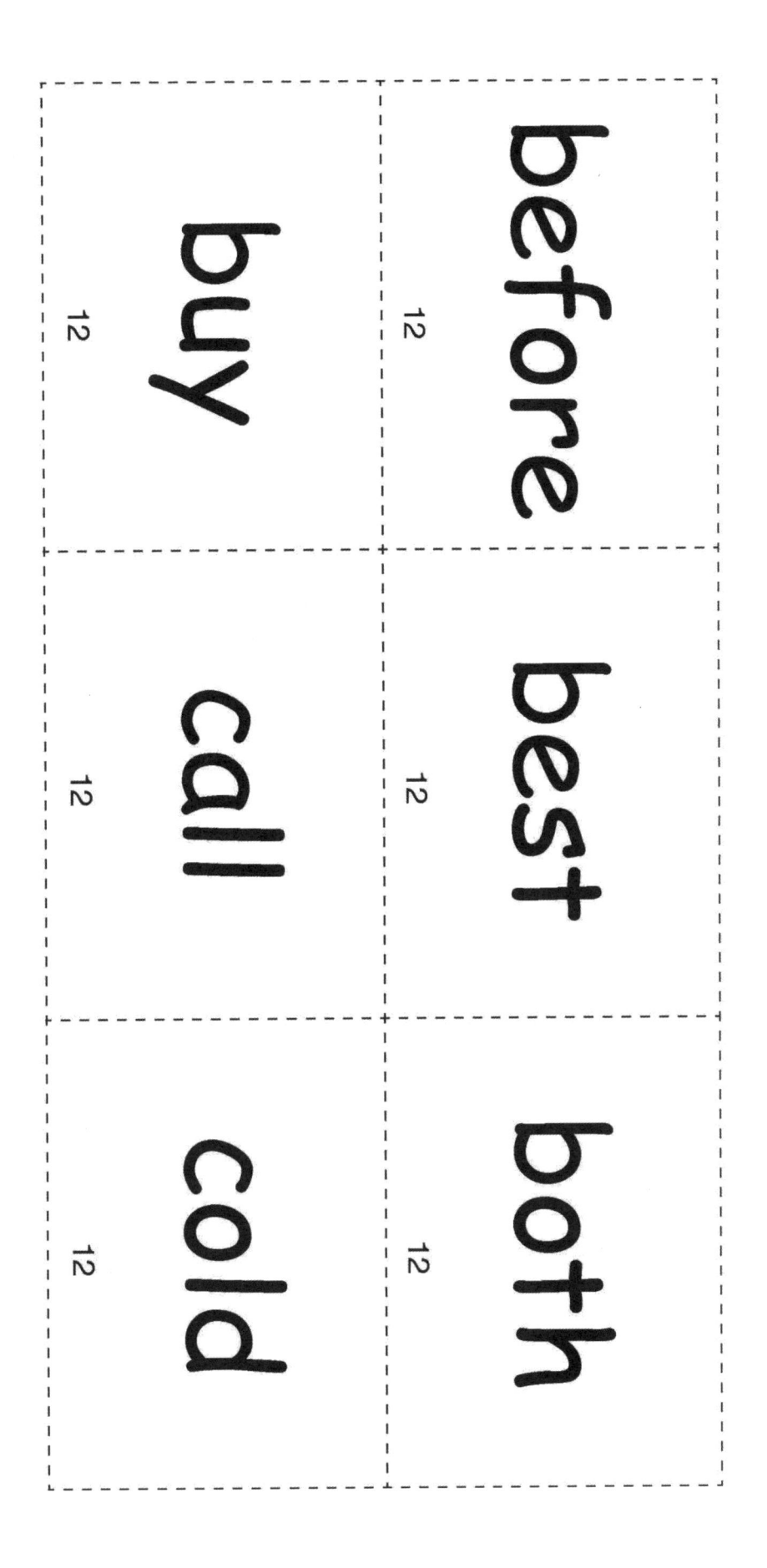

12.1 - Night Animals

Sight Words - *Rural vs. City*
Sight Word Cards

Here are your sight words for this lesson. Cut out these flashcards along the dotted lines. Add these to your word wall.

Cut them out!

does	fast	first
13	13	13

five	found	gave
13	13	13

Continue on the following page.

Flashcards

13.1 - Rural vs. City

343

goes	green	its
made	many	off

13.1 - Rural vs. City

Sight Words - *Jobs in the Community*

Sight Word Cards

Here are your sight words for this lesson. Cut out these flashcards along the dotted lines. Add these to your word wall.

Cut them out!

or	pull	read
14	14	14
right	sit	sleep
14	14	14

Continue on the following page.

14.1 - Jobs in the Community

tell	those
their	upon
these	sing

14.1 - Jobs in the Community

Sight Words - *Community Leaders*

Sight Word Cards

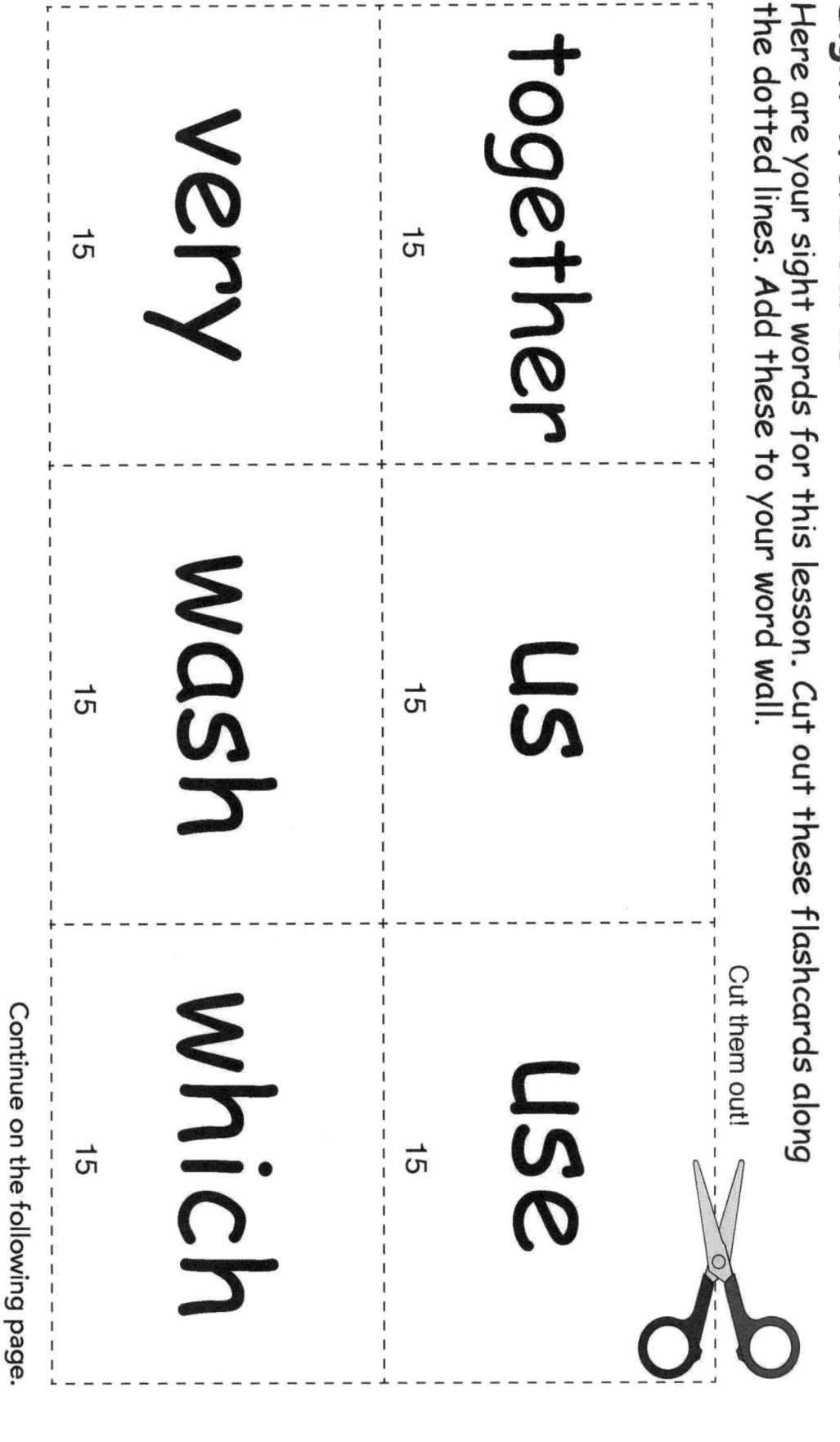

Here are your sight words for this lesson. Cut out these flashcards along the dotted lines. Add these to your word wall.

Cut them out!

Flashcards

together	us	use
15	15	15
very	wash	which
15	15	15

Continue on the following page.

15.1 - Community Leaders

why	wish	work
would	write	your

15.1 - Community Leaders

Sight Words - *The Presidency*

Sight Word Cards

Here are your sight words for this lesson. Cut out these flashcards along the dotted lines. Add these to your word wall.

Cut them out!

don't	better	bring
16	16	16
carry	clean	cut
16	16	16

Continue on the following page.

Flashcards

done	draw	drink
eight	fall	far

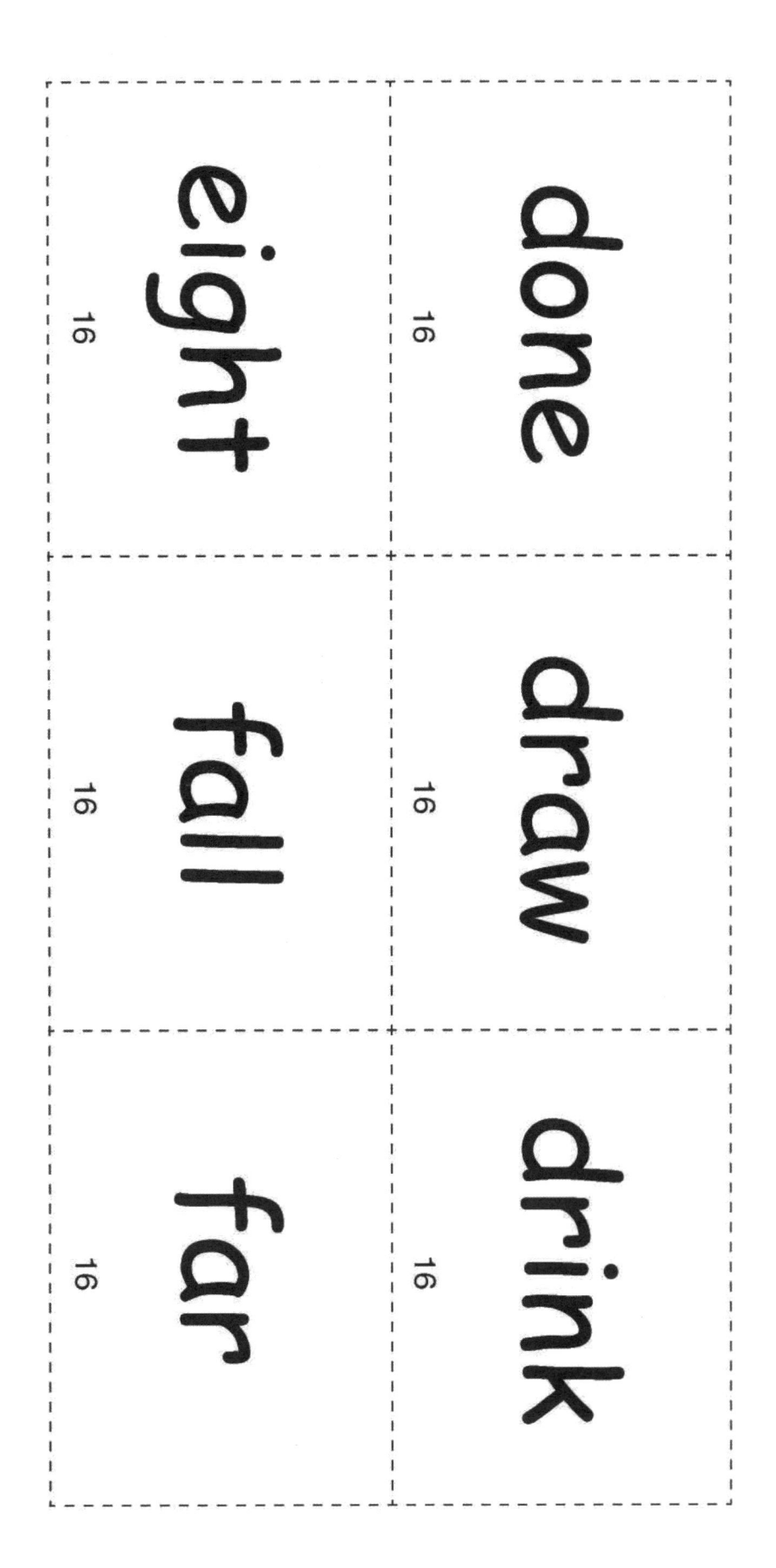

Sight Words – Winter Holidays Around the World

Sight Word Cards

Here are your sight words for this lesson. Cut out these flashcards along the dotted lines. Add these to your word wall.

Cut them out!

full	got	grow
hold	hot	hurt

Continue on the following page.

if	keep	kind
laugh	long	try

17.1 - Winter Holidays Around the World

Sight Words - *Time and New Years*

Sight Word Cards

Here are your sight words for this lesson. Cut out these flashcards along the dotted lines. Add these to your word wall.

Cut them out!

Flashcards

much	myself	never
18	18	18
only	own	pick
18	18	18

Continue on the following page.

18.1 - Time and New Years

363

seven	shall	show
six	small	start